Missionaries

The Inner-City Homeless Adventure

Reverend John Paul Emmanuel

Valentine Publishing House
Denver, Colorado

For more information about special discounts or bulk purchases, please contact Valentine Publishing House at 1-877-266-5289.

Publisher's Cataloging-in-Publication Data
　　Missionaries / Reverend John Paul Emmanuel.
　　Volume Two / The Inner-City Homeless Adventure.

　　p. cm.

　　LCCN: 2023951971
　　ISBN-10: 0-9994908-2-6
　　ISBN-13: 978-0-9994908-2-2

　　1. Christian Fiction.
　　2. Spiritual Warfare.
　　3. Evangelization.

　　PS3562.A315R44 2024
　　813'.54—dc22
　　2023951971

Printed in the United States of America.

The seventy returned with joy, saying,
"Lord, in your name even the demons submit to us!"
He said to them, "I watched Satan fall from
heaven like a flash of lightning. See, I have given
you authority to tread on snakes and scorpions,
and over all the power of the enemy; and nothing
will hurt you. Nevertheless, do not rejoice at this,
that the spirits submit to you, but rejoice that
your names are written in heaven."

Luke 10:17–20

1st CHAPTER

Missionaries

While the missionaries were attending Sunday brunch at the Luxembourg Hotel, Doctor David Bennett and his wife were expecting to arrive at Jubilee Fellowship Church a few minutes late. They were traveling on University Boulevard, when all of a sudden, a gray minivan entered the intersection traveling around sixty miles per hour.

"Distort his vision," a demonic spirit said.

Because the driver of the minivan thought he had a green light, he didn't even slow down. The minivan was traveling directly in line with the morning sun when it struck Doctor Bennett's car behind the driver's front door. The impact was devastating. Broken glass and mangled car parts were scattered all over the intersection.

After the paramedics arrived to rush Martha Bennett to the hospital, Overwatch dispatched an assignment of angels to escort the soul of Doctor David Bennett to his heavenly mansion.

When the demonic entities returned to their base of operations, Phantalon said, "Give me a report."

"The assignment has been accomplished," one of the demonic spirits said. "We distorted the sunlight that was reflecting off the glass lens, making the green light appear brighter than the red light."

"Well done," Phantalon said.

* * *

Later that week, when the missionaries were planning to meet at Holy Trinity Catholic Parish for Jclub's weekly business meeting, Daniel arrived first in his black BMW 7-Series and unlocked the basement door.

Michelle arrived next in her white four-door Jeep. She began by making cinnamon tea and placed the blueberry muffins that her mother had baked on a serving platter. Matthew arrived a few minutes later in his silver Toyota 4Runner and greeted Father O'Connor in the parking lot.

"Did you receive a package for me?" Father asked.

"Let me check with Daniel downstairs," Matthew said. "I thought there was a cardboard box sitting in front of the storage room doors."

When Matthew and Father O'Connor walked down the stairs, Michelle ran over to greet her fiancé with a hug and kiss. She turned to Father and said, "We're getting married," as she extended her hand to show him the diamond engagement ring.

"Congratulations," Father said. "Do you have a date in mind?"

"Ever since I was a little girl, I have dreamed about a beach wedding," Michelle said. "In my dreams, there's a white shade canopy decorated with lace, surrounded by tropical flowers and chairs in a semi-circular pattern facing the ocean. We would want warmer weather for the wedding, so sometime in June or July would be perfect."

"I'm not sure the Catholic Church will conduct a beach wedding," Matthew said.

"That's correct," Father O'Connor said. "Because marriage is a Sacrament, a sacred union between the married couple and God, it can only occur within a church during Mass, between two baptized adults who are in full communion with the Catholic Church."

"I'm not Catholic," Michelle said.

"We can fix that," Father said. "I will sign you up for RCIA classes in the fall. After you come into full communion with the Church during the Easter services, you can get married sometime next year."

"What are RCIA classes?" Michelle asked.

"It stands for Rite of Christian Initiation for Adults," Matthew said.

"There's my package," Father O'Connor said as he picked up a cardboard box that was sitting on the floor. "I don't know why they deliver packages to the basement when the parish office is open three days a week."

After Father O'Connor turned to leave, Michelle took a seat at a cafeteria-style table next to Daniel, who was working on his laptop computer.

"What's wrong?" Matthew asked.

"We never discussed any of this," Michelle said. "I was hoping we could start planning our wedding together. I'm picturing a tropical island with white sandy beaches along with a romantic sunset, followed by a late-night bonfire. Then out of nowhere, you and Reverend O'Connor want to convert me to Catholicism."

"This is a good example of the spiritual alignment phase that we spoke about," Matthew said. "All we need to do is work together with God through prayer, listening to each other, learning, growing and making a few compromises together."

"I don't think I should be a part of this conversation," Daniel said.

"We can talk about this later," Matthew said. "It's more important that we work through the details to transfer the office of president to Daniel so that we can leave on our first mission trip to Africa."

"I think we need to finish our conversation about marriage," Michelle said.

"Because fifty percent of all marriages end in a painful divorce, the Catholic Church wants to make sure couples are fully prepared to enter into a lifetime commitment together," Matthew said. "Because marriage is a sacred union between the couple and God, the Church wants to make sure couples are baptized spirit-filled Christians who can enter into the serious nature of that commitment.

"In addition, I think the Church needs to take the

RCIA process one step further to make sure couples have God's permission and approval to get married."

"If you want me to be a part of this conversation," Daniel said, "just because a religious leader says that it would be okay for Rebecca and I to get married, that doesn't mean we would have God's approval. I'm sure it would be possible to get married in any number of churches without God's permission or approval, but without the power of the Holy Spirit to help couples get through the difficult times, I'm sure every one of those relationships would experience difficulties."

"I agree that we need God's permission to get married," Michelle said, "but what does that have to do with me renouncing my Southern Baptist faith and becoming Catholic?"

"There may be an exemption," Matthew said. "I remember reading a section in the *Catechism* about mixed marriages between Catholics and non-Catholics.[1] There's also a section in the *Code of Canon Law* that describes secret marriages with private records that are kept in the Bishop's office."[2]

"Do you want me to search for that information on the Internet?" Daniel asked.

"Thank you," Michelle said.

"There are several sections under the heading of mixed marriages that require the permission of a Bishop," Daniel said. "Do you want me to research those requirements?"

"Yes, please," Michelle said.

"I have an appointment at eleven o'clock," Matthew said. "Let's draft the paperwork to make Daniel the new president of Jclub. I would like to meet at the Château Coffee Company tonight around seven o'clock to sign the resolution; then afterward, we can make a public announcement."

"That's a great idea," Michelle said. "Do you think Rebecca will be able to join us?"

"I hope so," Daniel said. "I will call her right now."

* * *

When Matthew and Michelle arrived at the Château Coffee Company, they greeted Daniel and Rebecca, who were socializing with several other Jclub members near the fireplace in the lounge area.

"We have over seventy members present tonight," Daniel said. "I invited everyone who would answer their phone."

"Let me know when you're ready to make the announcement," Michelle said. "I will ask the owners to turn down the music."

After the entire room fell silent, Matthew stood next to Michelle and said, "Thank you for attending Jclub's meet and greet tonight. This is a special night of celebration because over the weekend, Michelle accepted my marriage proposal, and Jclub has a new president. I'm sure everybody knows Daniel as a hard-working, highly motivated businessman, so we made him the new president of Jclub. Meanwhile, Michelle and I will be traveling to Africa to conduct short-term mission trips."

After a brief moment of silence, everybody at the Château Coffee Company lifted up a generous amount of applause while the owners offered free drinks to all the guests for the rest of the evening. After the announcement, Michelle was surrounded by a circle of her friends who wanted to hear the details and see her engagement ring. Daniel and Rebecca received what seemed to be an endless outpouring of congratulations that evening, while Matthew engaged a group of Jclub members who were interested in learning more about his plans to visit Africa.

"Everybody is welcome to join us on a short-term mission trip," Matthew said.

"What country are you planning to visit?" one of the Jclub members asked.

"I'm not sure," Matthew said. "I'm feeling called to minister to Muslims, so I have been praying about locations closest to Saudi Arabia, such as Libya, Egypt, Sudan or even Somalia."

"I admire your courage," one of the Jclub members said, "but all of those countries would be way too dangerous for me and my girlfriend."

"Somalia is one of the most dangerous countries in the world," another Jclub member said. "I don't think they have a functioning government. Sudan has been fighting a long and drawn out civil war, and it wasn't that long ago that the United States military removed Muammar Gaddafi from power in Libya."

"I also wanted to visit some other countries that

speak English," Matthew said, "such as Liberia, Ghana, Nigeria and Kenya."

"It still sounds way too dangerous for me," another Jclub member said. "Doesn't Nigeria have an Islamic terrorist group called Boko Haram that kidnaps schoolchildren? I think their name stands for *no western education*. There's also a town in the center of Nigeria called Jos where Christians and Muslims fight each other with machetes. At least once a year a riot breaks out and hundreds of people are either killed or wounded."

"In some countries, such as Iran, Iraq and Saudi Arabia, they will arrest anyone who is caught with Christian literature," another Jclub member said. "Many missionaries who visit those places have been accused of speaking blasphemies against the Prophet Muhammad and are sentenced to death, or worse, tortured in one of their detention facilities."

"That's why it's so important to pray and ask God questions about our missionary activities," Matthew said. "As Christians, we have direct access to God's throne. We can spend time in silence, practicing contemplative prayer and discerning the Lord's will for our lives. We need to hear very clearly from God so that we don't get outside of the Lord's will for our lives and end up being hurt."

"Good point," another Jclub member said.

At the end of the evening, Daniel approached Matthew and Michelle with Rebecca at his side and said, "Rebecca and I would like to invite you to a grand opening at the Summit View Cafe on Friday night."

"It's located a few blocks away from Bethany Christian College," Rebecca said.

"Isn't that on the other side of town," Matthew asked, "about an hour away?"

"I know it's a long drive," Daniel said, "but we wanted to expand operations and increase our territory."

"That's a great idea," Michelle said. "We would love to attend."

*   *   *

The Summit View Cafe was located on top of an elevated plateau overlooking a small college town. It was a popular hangout for cyclists, and the interior of the cafe was decorated with an assortment of antique bicycles that were suspended from the ceiling.

When Friday night arrived, Michelle reached the destination an hour early to help Daniel and Rebecca set up a table with sales brochures and new membership applications. When Matthew arrived an hour later, he greeted Michelle with a kiss and said, "I have some very bad news to share with you."

"What's wrong?" Michelle asked. "You look tired. Are you feeling okay?"

"I have been trying to get in contact with Doctor Bennett for the past several days, but his phone has been turned off. When I stopped by his house, his brother told me there was an accident early Sunday morning. Doctor Bennett and his wife were on their way to church when a minivan ran a red light. The police haven't made any arrests, but when they visited the property where the minivan was registered, the owner wanted to report the vehicle as stolen."

"Oh, no," Michelle said.

After a long moment of silence, Matthew said, "The paramedics rushed Martha to the hospital, where she survived a few more hours on life support before she passed away. Doctor Bennett went to be with the Lord immediately after the minivan ripped through the side of his car."

"I'm so sorry," Michelle said. "Is there anything I can do?"

"The funeral will be held at Jubilee Fellowship Church next week," Matthew said.

After sensing the pain that Matthew was experiencing, Michelle wrapped her arms around him for a long time as she rested her head against his chest without saying a word. After a long moment of silence, Matthew said, "Will you please explain the situation to Daniel and Rebecca at an appropriate time, maybe at the end of the evening, and extend my apologies for not being able to participate in their grand opening? I just want to go home and be alone."

"I will stop by your place tomorrow morning," Michelle said as Matthew slowly walked away.

* * *

The next morning, when Michelle knocked on Matthew's door, she was holding a bag of groceries. When he opened the door, she said, "I want to make egg white omelets, so I brought some yellow bell peppers, tomatoes, chives and shredded cheddar cheese."

"I'm not hungry," Matthew said.

"That's okay," Michelle said. "Do you have any butter?"

As Michelle was working in the kitchen, Matthew took a seat at the kitchen table and said, "I'm experiencing a lot of resistance trying to find a Christian ministry that specializes in delivering the Gospel message to Muslims. There's only one ministry on the Internet that claims to minister to Muslims, but when I call, they won't give me any information. They treat me like an Islamic spy who only wants the information to attack their ministry efforts."

"Do you remember the missionaries who were kidnapped in Haiti and held for ransom?" Michelle asked. "They advertised all of their outreach activities, dates and locations on the Internet for the purpose of raising financial support. All the kidnappers had to do was search the Internet for 'American mission trips to Haiti' to know the exact dates and times where the kidnap victims would be located."

"That would be a painful lesson to learn the hard way," Matthew said. "I'm sure it would be equally as dangerous trying to advertise a Christian outreach for Muslims on the Internet."

"I'm going to put extra cheese on your omelet," Michelle said.

"I'm also getting a lot of resistance from Christian

ministries that don't want anything to do with Muslims," Matthew said. "When I called several evangelical organizations in Liberia looking for a driver who could pick us up from the airport, they got all nasty with me. I made international calls for over an hour and was only able to acquire a telephone number for a taxi driver who wanted a hundred dollars per day to drive us around."

"It sounds like you're experiencing a major roadblock in regards to our trip to Africa," Michelle said.

"Then to make matters worse, not only did we lose a good friend, Christian elder and mentor, but we also lost all of our funding," Matthew said.

As Michelle was serving the omelets, she said, "I know this may sound cliché, but when the Lord closes one door, he always opens another. Although I'm still feeling called to visit Africa, I'm wondering if we should reconsider the timing. Maybe there's something we need to accomplish in America before we go."

"We still need to get all our shots," Matthew said. "I started making calls to travel clinics last week, and we need about five hundred dollars worth of shots. It's important that we get our hepatitis A and B, yellow fever, typhoid and meningococcal shots.

"It's also a good idea to get booster shots for polio, measles, mumps and rubella since those diseases are more prevalent in the countries that we will be visiting. I didn't want to get all those shots at the same time, so maybe it's a blessing that we have time to prepare."

"We could also use this time of preparation to strengthen our personal relationship," Michelle said.

"What do you mean?" Matthew asked.

"It would seem that an essential part of the RCIA process would be to make sure engaged couples maintain similar views of the Catholic faith," Michelle said. "Because I have several concerns regarding the Catholic Church, it may be a good idea for us to work through those issues during this time of preparation, so that we can more effectively minister together in Africa."

"What kind of concerns?" Matthew asked.

"All the usual anti-Catholic concerns that a girl my age would hear about growing up in a Southern Baptist church her entire life," Michelle said. "For example, call no man your father, infant baptism, purgatory, and confessing your sins to a man in a tiny dark room. In addition, I have questions about the veneration of saints and praying endless rosaries to the Mary statue over and over again."

"I will prepare a Biblically based explanation for all your concerns," Matthew said. "Should I work on this before or after I find a new job?"

"I'm sorry," Michelle said. "I know you are going through a difficult time right now, but I feel we are on the verge of a major breakthrough. Sometimes it's necessary to travel through the dark valley of pain and hardships before we can experience the joy of a mountaintop experience. All we need to do is press hard into the Lord, seek his will for our lives, and listen to the Holy

Spirit's softly spoken voice."

"Thank you for the encouragement," Matthew said. "I will get very serious in prayer and ask God to remove anything in my life that's not pleasing to him. I want Jesus to stretch me past my limits, break me down and rebuild me into the man he wants me to be, so we can embark on the next level of our journey together."

"If it's okay with you, I would like to keep working as the event coordinator for Jclub until we figure out the next stage of our journey," Michelle said as she opened the front door, gave Matthew a kiss goodbye and left.

* * *

The following afternoon, Michelle stopped by Matthew's apartment to see how he was doing. Because it took him a while to answer the door, she said, "I think you should give me a key to your apartment so that I can let myself in any time I want. If we are going to get married, we should have greater access to each other's lives."

"I will get a key made for you," Matthew said.

"I have some great news to share with you, and it couldn't wait," Michelle said. "I spoke to my friend Elizabeth, who knows a chaplain at the Parkside Rescue Mission. They have an opening for a weekday afternoon chapel service provider. They are looking for a powerful street preacher, and you would be perfect."

"I don't know anything about being a street preacher," Matthew said.

"At least meet with him," Michelle said. "His name

is Chaplain Hemingway, and I have his phone number."

"How much does it pay?" Matthew asked.

"It's a volunteer position, so it only pays heavenly treasure," Michelle said, "although the potential for additional ministry opportunities is endless."

"I still don't think it's a good idea," Matthew said.

"Why not?" Michelle asked. "You haven't had time to pray about it. Let's seek the Lord's will for our lives regarding this golden opportunity."

"It feels like my life has been destroyed," Matthew said. "I don't feel like doing anything right now."

"That's why this is the perfect opportunity for you," Michelle said. "As your fiancée, it's my job to provide all the support and encouragement that you need. So if it's okay with you, I will call Chaplain Hemingway and set an appointment for us tomorrow morning so we can take a tour of the facility to see if it would be a good match for us."

"Very well," Matthew said, "except I don't have any experience working with the homeless."

"I will call you with the proposed meeting time," Michelle said, giving Matthew a kiss goodbye.

2nd CHAPTER

The Parkside Rescue Mission was located in one of the most dangerous parts of town known as *skid row*. The sidewalks and back alleyways were populated with drug addicts, drug dealers, prostitutes, alcoholics and dangerous criminals who had just been released from prison.

When Matthew and Michelle arrived for their appointment, there was a line of at least thirty homeless men and women sitting on the sidewalk on the north side of the building.

"I'm feeling a little over-dressed for our job interview," Michelle said as they passed through a steel door and approached a security station that was enclosed behind bulletproof glass.

After the missionaries introduced themselves, the man behind the glass said, "Please have a seat in the chapel." Then he pressed a button to release the locking mechanism on the exterior door.

When Chaplain Hemingway arrived, he said,

"Delighted to make your acquaintance. Elizabeth told me all about the great work that you have been doing at Jclub. She said you're an excellent preacher, a powerful evangelist, and that you have a love and heart for ministering to the youth."

"You're too kind," Matthew said. "This is my fiancée, Michelle."

"It's lovely to make your acquaintance," Michelle said.

"We serve three meals per day at the Rescue Mission, and all of our guests are required to attend a chapel service before each meal is served," the Chaplain said. "At eleven o'clock in the morning, we open the exterior doors and fill the chapel to capacity for the afternoon service.

"We usually provide a half-hour chapel service of preaching that contains the Gospel message before sending the first group downstairs to our cafeteria, where everybody is served a hot meal. Once the chapel empties out, we will open the exterior doors again and start the process over again until everybody has been served."

"How many times do you fill the room?" Matthew asked.

"The chapel holds about one hundred and twenty guests," the Chaplain said. "When it's warm and sunny outside, we usually fill the room once, but when it's freezing cold or rainy outside, we could easily fill the chapel two or three times."

"If it's cold and rainy and we need to conduct three

chapel services that day, would the service times range from eleven o'clock in the morning to one o'clock in the afternoon?" Michelle asked.

"You are welcome to stay longer if you want to personally minister to any of our guests," the Chaplain said.

"Do you also provide overnight sleeping arrangements for your guests?" Matthew asked.

"We have lavatory and shower facilities, along with a hundred and eighty cots on the second floor that are available on a first-come, first-served basis," he said.

"How does your application and approval process work?" Matthew asked.

"You're already approved," Chaplain Hemingway said. "From all the great things that Elizabeth has told me about your ministry, I can't wait to hear you preach."

"Are you looking for someone five days a week?" Michelle asked.

"Because we don't have a weekday afternoon service provider, I have been playing religious movies for our guests," the Chaplain said. "Then right before the meal is served, I will come back to pray with the audience before sending them downstairs to eat lunch."

"Would it be possible to volunteer three days a week?" Matthew asked. "I was thinking about Monday, Wednesday and Friday. I wanted to give it a try so that we could pray and discern if this is something we are being called to do on a regular basis."

"That would be great," the Chaplain said.

"How do you receive your sermon ideas?" Matthew asked.

"My best sermons have always come from my interactions with our guests," Chaplain Hemingway said. "When I spend time with the homeless population, I start to feel what they are feeling. When I connect with the hardships and struggles they are experiencing on a daily basis, I know exactly what message they need to hear from the pulpit.

"Because there's always an overwhelming sense of

hopelessness and spiritual darkness in the room, I try to find creative ways to bring stories from the Bible alive in a way that imparts God's love, hope and new life in Christ. I also close every message with a call-to-action and a prayer where the audience has the opportunity to repent of their sins and accept Jesus as their personal Lord and Savior."

"This sounds like the perfect opportunity for us," Michelle said.

"When can we start?" Matthew asked.

"Anytime you want," Chaplain Hemingway said.

"How about Friday?" Matthew said. "That will give us a few days to prepare a message."

After the missionaries finished taking a tour of the facility, they went outside to talk with a few homeless men and women who were seated on the sidewalk.

"Let's sit down next to them so we can feel what they are experiencing," Matthew said.

After taking a seat on the sidewalk next to a home-less man, Michelle asked, "What's everyone in line for?"

"I don't know," the homeless man said. "I just sat down because everybody else was kicking back."

"How long have you been on the streets?" Matthew asked.

"My entire life," the homeless man said. "Ever since I lost my job at the steel plant and got divorced, every-thing has been a downward spiral."

"Do you ever reach out to God for help?" Matthew asked.

"It's God's fault that I'm in this situation," the homeless man said. "I used to pray every day, but not anymore."

"Is it okay if we pray for you?" Michelle asked.

"You can do anything you want," the homeless man said. "Just keep your religion and your God away from me."

"If you tell us your name, we will pray for you every day this week," Michelle said.

"My name is Jack Emerson," the man said.

"It's good to meet you," Matthew said. "This is my fiancée, Michelle. We're coming back here for the Friday afternoon chapel service, so if we see you around, I would like to take you out to lunch afterward. It would be my treat. We could order some burgers and fries, or maybe even a fried chicken dinner."

"That would be great," Jack said.

"I'm looking forward to our time together on Friday," Michelle said, waving goodbye.

As the missionaries were walking back to Matthew's 4Runner parked in the lot across the street, he said, "That was easy. I know exactly what to preach about on Friday."

"I'm so happy you are willing to give this a try," Michelle said. "You're a gifted evangelist, and these guys are going to be drawn to your strength. I know you will be able to deliver a powerful message that will motivate the audience into a deeper and more intimate relationship with Jesus."

"Thank you for the encouragement," Matthew said. "There was something about Chaplain Hemingway that set my heart on fire during our meeting."

"The Holy Spirit was also ministering to my heart," Michelle said. "That's why I need to go shopping at a thrift store for the latest homeless fashions so that I blend in better."

* * *

After the demonic entities that had been following the missionaries discovered their plans, they reported back to Phantalon and said, "There's a flop house in Narco-Leóna's territory. Members of her security detail made it clear that we were not welcome in the area, so we told them we were conducting a reconnaissance mission, and they wanted you to report directly to Narco-Leóna to give her the details."

"From what we have ascertained, the missionaries have cancelled their trip to Africa and are planning to rehabilitate gutter-punks and whiskey-pigs on skid row," another demon said.

"I will deal with Narco-Leóna directly," Phantalon said as he departed through the roof of the farmhouse.

When Phantalon entered into Narco-Leóna's territory, he was confronted by a security detail that escorted him into Narco-Leóna's presence.

"What are you doing here?" Narco-Leóna asked as she confronted the intruder.

"There's a group of monkeys that have caused me to experience a great loss," Phantalon said. "They were able to call down an assignment of angelic warriors that destroyed my entire operation. We were able to cut off their financial donations, but they have plans to evangelize your flophouse."

"Your principality was destroyed because your minions are weak," Narco-Leóna said. "My only concern is for the real estate developers who are constantly buying up my abandoned warehouses and converting my territory into high-rise apartments. They fill those lofts with residents who are constantly complaining and causing all kinds of problems with government officials. If the remains of your principality can stop the real estate developers from consuming any more of my territory, I would be interested in working with you."

"I only want to see the monkeys destroyed," Phantalon said. "Out of great respect for the work that you have accomplished here, I just wanted to warn you about their existence."

"We have been dealing with twelve steppers who visit the flophouse for many years," Narco-Leóna said. "I can assure you, they will not last very long. We will set a trap for them, and after they are destroyed, you and your minions will be better off working for me."

"I will consider your most gracious offer," Phantalon said, departing through the roof of the abandoned building.

* * *

When the missionaries returned to the Parkside Rescue Mission for the Friday afternoon service,

Michelle started working the front door as a greeter to make sure everybody felt welcomed, while Matthew set up the microphone and played a CD with soft inspirational music. When the room was filled to capacity, Michelle closed the outside door and Matthew began his message by saying, "Please turn with me to the Book of Job. If you need a Bible, please raise your hand, and Michelle will give you one.

"Job was a wealthy man who owned seven thousand sheep, three thousand camels and five hundred yoke of oxen. The Bible says Job was the richest and most successful man of his day.[3] Job was also a Godly man—one who was blameless and upright—a man who loved the Lord and turned away from evil.

"The Bible also says that the Lord established a hedge of protection around Job and all that he owned.[4] In the spiritual realm, this hedge of protection looked like an invisible force field that surrounded him at all times. It was a supernatural canopy of protection where the Lord blessed the work of Job's hands, so that his possessions increased in the land.

"Then one day Satan went before the Lord and accused Job of receiving special treatment. Satan claimed that Job was being overly protected and blessed for no apparent reason. Because Satan hated Job, he wanted to destroy him, but because God had established a spiritual hedge of protection around Job at all times, the devil could not touch him.

"After God granted the devil permission to attack

Job, we see Satan causing an accident that killed all of his children. In verse nineteen, Job's children were eating and drinking in the eldest brother's house when a great wind swept across the desert. The forces of nature, driven by the powers of the demonic, struck the four corners of the home so that it fell on Job's children and everybody inside the house died.[5]

"We also see Satan attacking Job's finances. An assignment of fallen angels motivated a group of armed bandits to make a raid on Job's camels, oxen and donkeys. They killed his servants with their swords and stole all his livestock. Then to make matters worse, Satan inflicted loathsome sores on Job from the soles of his feet to the crown of his head.[6]

"This is a good example of demonic illness. The Bible provides many other examples of demonic illness. For example, there was a time when Jesus cast a demonic spirit out of a crippled woman who wasn't able to stand up straight.[7] She was immediately healed and started praising God. There was also a boy who suffered from seizures.[8] When Jesus cast a demonic spirit out of the child, he recovered.

"We can see from all these examples that Satan, along with his vast army of fallen angels, can cause accidents, sickness and disease. In John, chapter ten, the Bible says that Satan only has one purpose—to steal, kill and destroy.[9]

"After thinking about all these examples, I'm wondering if there are some men and women in the audience today who can relate to Job. Maybe at one point in your past you were wealthy. Maybe you owned a nice house, had a great job and drove a nice car, then one day the devil came along and staged an attack, causing a series of losses until there was nothing left to lose. If the devil has destroyed your life in the same way that he destroyed Job's life, do you think it would be appropriate to get angry and blame God?"

After Matthew asked the audience this question, a homeless man seated in the back of the room shouted out, "It's God's fault for allowing the devil to exist!" Other men in the audience said that the devil was to blame. Because arguments were starting to break out in the audience, Matthew continued his message by saying, "To settle this debate, we need to look at the purpose of our lives.

"If the purpose of life is to be wealthy and have fun, then I would say God was at fault for allowing the devil to destroy Job's life; but what if the purpose of life is not to be wealthy and have fun? What if the purpose of this life is nothing more than a test that will determine our status in God's eternal kingdom?

"In Job's situation, God allowed the devil's attack to see if Job would pass the test. After the devil destroyed Job's health, family and finances, we see Job's response in verse twenty—he fell to the ground and worshiped. 'In all this Job did not sin or charge God with wrongdoing.'[10]

"After Job passed the test, we see God blessing the

later days of Job more than in his beginning. The Bible says that God restored to Job fourteen thousand sheep, six thousand camels and a thousand yoke of oxen. He had seven other sons and three daughters, lived one hundred and forty years and died old and full of days.[11]

"In the same way that Job had a choice to make, every person in this room also has a choice to make: We can get angry and blame God, or we can fall to the ground and worship. We have a loving God who can put a hedge of protection around us and all that we own so that our possessions will increase in the land, or we can get angry at God and allow the devil to continue his cycle of destruction.

"The choice is yours! What choice do you want to make? If you want God to restore your life, please come forward after the service. I would like to pray with you. The rest of the audience can proceed downstairs for a hot meal."

After Matthew offered an invitation for prayer, twenty-one men and several women came forward for prayer. He continued his message to the smaller group of men and women by saying, "The only way you can enter into an authentic relationship with God is by accepting Jesus' sacrifice on the cross for the forgiveness of your sins.

"Once your sins have been forgiven, we can pray together to receive the gift of the Holy Spirit. After you invite the Holy Spirit to dwell in your life and heart, you can start working in partnership with God to restore all that the devil has stolen. Step by step, you will be able to accomplish God's will in your life."

After ministering to the group for over an hour, the missionaries made sure everybody had accepted Jesus' sacrifice on the cross for the forgiveness of their sins. They also prayed with the men and women to be filled with the Holy Spirit so that they could begin the process of restoring all that the devil had stolen.

After everybody left the chapel and went downstairs to receive a hot meal, Michelle said, "That was an excellent message. I like how you engaged the audience and captured everybody's attention."

"Thank you for the encouragement," Matthew said. "Preaching to this audience is very draining. I could feel a lot of resistance in the back of the room. It felt dark and heavy, as if there's a lot of demonic oppression going on with these guys."

"Maybe you could preach about that topic at the next service," Michelle said.

"Good idea," Matthew said. "Let me walk you to your Jeep. It's a dangerous neighborhood around here, and I don't want you coming down here by yourself."

* * *

After the service ended, the demonic spirits that had been assigned to the Rescue Mission reported back to Narco-Leóna and said, "You should have heard all the bad things that monkey was saying about us. He was able to captivate the whiskey-pigs' attention, and we were powerless to stop him."

"Stir up a controversy with the staff members who work at the flophouse," Narco-Leóna said. "Get them to expel the preacher over differences in their religious doctrine. You should also motivate the wine-babblers in the back of the room to start fighting with each other while he is preaching."

* * *

The next day, Matthew stopped by the church basement to see how Daniel was doing. After walking down the stairs, he noticed a stack of cardboard boxes in the hallway. Because Daniel was busy inside the storage room loading more boxes with files, Matthew asked, "What's going on?"

"I rented an executive suite at the Paramount Plaza Center," Daniel said. "It's located on the twenty-seventh floor with an incredible view of the downtown area. I can't wait to show it to you."

"It sounds very expensive," Matthew said.

"I rented the smallest suite available," Daniel said. "It's only one hundred and twenty square feet, but it feels very impressive. When clients visit our new office, they will pass through two eight-foot-tall frosted glass doors and be greeted by a full-time receptionist.

"There's an elegant waiting area with modern furnishings and a huge conference room. The layout will make our clients feel like they're visiting a Fortune 500 company, but in reality, we're only renting a small room in the back corner for a very reasonable price."

As Matthew and Daniel were discussing Jclub's new

office, a young lady walked down the stairs and said, "Is there anybody down here?"

"How can I help you?" Matthew asked, looking around the corner.

"It has been a while," the young lady said. "Do you remember me? My name is Judy. I used to be a Jclub member several years ago. I stopped coming to your events after I got married, but now I'm divorced."

"It's good to see you again," Matthew said. "I'm no longer involved with the leadership at Jclub, but I would like to introduce you to our new president."

"When I was driving by, I felt the Holy Spirit's inspiration to stop by and talk with you," Judy said. "I just bought a house, and I need to build a privacy fence in the back yard to keep my kids safe. I remembered that you had some construction experience, and I wanted to see if you could help me."

"I haven't worked construction in a long time," Matthew said. "Right now, I'm in a transition period. I'm feeling called to minister to Muslims in Africa, but after taking an abrupt detour, I have found myself working with the homeless."

"How exciting," Judy said. "Will you please take a look at my back yard? My son just turned two years old, and my daughter is four. The neighborhood isn't the best, so I would like to build a privacy fence to provide a safe place for my children to play."

"How many feet of fence do you need to install?" Matthew asked.

"I'm not sure," Judy said. "After paying all the closing costs, I have twenty-eight hundred dollars that I could pay you right away."

"Let's set up a time to meet at the property and I will help you take some measurements," Matthew said.

"I need to get back to the office right now," Judy said. "Let me give you the lockbox combination, my phone number and the property address. That way, you can evaluate the situation at your convenience."

"I will stop by this afternoon and give you a call this evening," Matthew said.

3rd CHAPTER

Judy's new home was located in the Woodshire subdivision on South Jackson Street. The eleven-hundred-square-foot ranch was surrounded by a large barren lot. When Matthew used the lockbox combination to open the front door, it was apparent the property had been recently renovated for sale.

The small, rectangular-shaped home had a new linoleum floor in the bathroom, three bedrooms and a tiny kitchen with an electric stove. The back yard consisted mostly of weeds that had been mowed close to the ground, and it was apparent why Judy wanted to seal it off from the alleyway behind her new home.

When Matthew called Judy that evening, he said, "I could build a six-foot cedar privacy fence in the back yard for three thousand dollars."

"Thank you so much," Judy said. "I'm so grateful, and I was starting to get desperate. That's when I prayed and felt inspired to ask you for help."

"When do you plan to move in?" Matthew asked.

"I need to be out of my old house by the end of the month," Judy said.

"It shouldn't take us more than a few days," Matthew said. "We will start work on Monday and have it finished by Friday."

When Matthew called Michelle later that evening, he said, "I found the perfect opportunity to help some homeless guys. An old Jclub member named Judy just bought a house and she needs to build a fence in her back yard. I was thinking we could hire two homeless guys who have experience in construction to dig the post holes. Because the house is vacant, they could spend the night on the floor. If we buy the materials cheap enough, the project could provide them with enough money to rent their own apartments."

"My only concern would be the liability," Michelle said. "What would happen if someone got hurt?"

"It's not that hard to build a fence," Matthew said. "It's the perfect job for the homeless because it's outdoors and there's nothing around for them to screw up. All they need to do is dig some holes and I will help them set the posts. After the concrete dries, we can install the rails, and they can nail on the pickets. It's basically just using hand tools, so I'm sure they can handle it."

"I hope you're right about this," Michelle said.

* * *

At the end of the Monday afternoon chapel service, when the majority of the guests went downstairs to eat lunch, Matthew made an announcement to a smaller group of men by saying, "I would like to hire two guys with construction experience to help me build a fence. The job pays three thousand dollars, but with that money, we need to buy materials.

"The house where you will be working is vacant, so you will have a place to stay. If you work hard, and we shop around to buy the materials at the lowest possible price, there will be enough money left over for you to rent your own apartment. So for a few days of work, you can get off the streets and into your own place."

After making the announcement, about twenty men raised their hands, so Matthew conducted a careful evaluation and chose Randy and Barney. They both looked physically fit and assured him they could handle the job.

Later that day, Matthew dropped Randy and Barney off at the job site along with a wheelbarrow, a posthole digger and several shovels. He stayed long enough to mark the location of each posthole by driving a stake into the ground.

"You guys should have everything you need," Matthew said. "These holes need to be ten inches round and two feet deep. I will leave the back door of Judy's house open so that you can use the restroom and sleep on the floor tonight. I will come back and check on you first thing in the morning."

"Can we get an advance?" Randy asked.

"Don't you guys have any money?" Matthew asked.

"I'm totally broke," Barney said. "We just need a few bucks to buy some food for dinner."

"All I have is a fifty dollar bill," Matthew said, "so you guys will have to split it."

* * *

The next morning when Matthew drove over to Judy's house to inspect the work, none of the postholes had been completed except for one, which was only six inches deep. When Matthew went inside the house, it looked like the homeless guys tried to build a fire in the kitchen to keep themselves warm, because there was a pile of burnt newspaper ashes inside the oven.

Because Matthew could hear the sound of running water, he went into the bathroom and found the toilet plugged up with newspaper. The handle on the toilet was stuck open, allowing a steady stream of toilet water to spill over the rim and onto the new linoleum floor. Because the water had been seeping through the floor all night and draining into the basement, it caused the wooden underlayment on the new bathroom floor to buckle.

When he finally found Randy and Barney in the back alleyway getting drunk on vodka and beer, he said, "Let me guess what happened; you took the fifty dollars that I gave you and went directly to the liquor store. You got drunk, plugged up the toilet with newspaper, ruined the bathroom floor, flooded the basement with water, and then tried to build a fire inside the oven."

"Hey man, we didn't have any toilet paper and it

was cold outside," Randy said.

"You're both fired!" Matthew said. "If you don't leave this area immediately, I'm going to call the police and have you arrested for the destruction of private property and trespassing."

After Randy and Barney wandered away, Matthew spent the rest of the day cleaning up the mess that the homeless men had caused.

* * *

Later that evening, Michelle stopped by Matthew's apartment to see how he was doing. When he opened the door, she said, "Are you okay? Your phone has been turned off all day."

"I don't want to talk about it," Matthew said.

"I knew something bad was going to happen," Michelle said. "Did they fake a job site injury so their attorney could extort you for money?"

"I'm lucky they didn't burn down the whole house," Matthew said. "All I wanted to do was help them get off the streets, and they screwed everything up. It was the perfect opportunity. All they needed to do was work hard for a few days, and they could have earned enough money to rent their own apartments, but no, they had to get drunk and flood the basement with toilet water."

"You wouldn't believe all the crazy stories that I have heard at Al-Anon meetings," Michelle said. "They call alcoholism a disease, but a better description is the devil playing sock-puppet with God's beloved children."

"It has been a very painful learning experience for me," Matthew said. "In the past, when I would see a homeless man standing on the sidewalk holding a cardboard sign, I used to give him a few bucks to make myself feel better. Now I know better. Anytime you give a drug addict or an alcoholic money, they will spend it on getting high or drunk."

"What are you going to do about Judy's house?" Michelle asked.

"I'm going to finish the job," Matthew said. "I think the underlayment on the bathroom floor will settle back down once all the water evaporates. I will go back tomorrow to dig the postholes myself. Once the concrete dries, I will install the rails and pickets. I will keep working until the job is complete."

"I want you to promise me something," Michelle said. "It's a mutual promise that we can make together."

"What is it?" Matthew asked.

"I want you to promise me that you will never invite a homeless person, a drug addict or an alcoholic into your apartment to live with you," Michelle said. "The same rule will also apply to me. I will never invite a homeless person, a drug addict or an alcoholic to live with me inside my mother's house."

"Why is that so important to you?" Matthew asked.

"If you give a homeless person free shelter, free food and free bus tokens, they will still be in need, so there has to be more to helping the homeless than making them dependent on free handouts," Michelle said.

"You're right," Matthew said. "If we are going to help the homeless, we have to address the root cause of the problems that are preventing these men and women from becoming productive members of society. I also think we need to spend more time trying to discern the difference between the sheep and the goats. Let's find out who is serious about serving the Lord, so that we can focus our time, attention and resources on helping those individuals."

"I will also make a ministry resource list," Michelle said. "If we have a handout with all the shelters' contact information, anytime we meet someone who needs housing, all we need to do is give them the list with the shelters' names, addresses, phone numbers and services provided. We could also include traveler's resources just in case we meet someone who is stranded and needs to get back home. The resource list could also include food banks, food lines, detox facilities and employment resources."

"That's a great idea," Matthew said.

"I will work on the resource list tomorrow," Michelle said as she gave Matthew a kiss good night.

* * *

The next time Matthew was scheduled to preach at the Rescue Mission, he said to the audience, "Please turn with me to the Gospel of Luke. In the fifteenth chapter, there's a story about a very wealthy landowner who had two sons.[12]

"The Bible doesn't offer a description of the man's

property, but it might be helpful to picture a vast cattle ranch surrounded by a lush forest with meadows of wildflowers and flowing streams.

"The property owner and his sons have to work very hard to take care of the livestock, till the soil and harvest the crops, but it's a very peaceful and rewarding place to live. After living in harmony with God's creation for many years, the younger son asked his father to give him his share of the inheritance. Once the young man received the money, he traveled to a distant country so that he could party with the devil. The Bible says the young man 'squandered his property in dissolute living.'[13] My question for you today is: What do you think the term *dissolute living* means?"

Because everyone in the audience remained silent, Matthew went on to say, "I looked up the words in my study guide, and it means 'debauchery.' So what does the word *debauchery* mean?" Because nobody in the audience could answer the question, Matthew went on to say, "Other translations of the Bible say 'wild living,' but when I looked up the word *debauchery* in the dictionary, it means 'excessive indulgences in sensual pleasures.'

"In Saint Paul's letter to the Ephesians, he says, 'Do not get drunk with wine, for that is debauchery.'[14] Verse thirty also gives us a deeper insight into the meaning of debauchery by saying the young man devoured the father's 'property with prostitutes.'[15]

"After the young man spent all his money partying with the devil—getting drunk, smoking pot, doing drugs and having sex with prostitutes—the Bible says a severe famine took place in that country and he began to be in need.[16]

"Because the young man found himself homeless and without any money, he hired himself out for day labor, and eventually someone sent him to a field to feed the pigs. He would have gladly eaten the garbage the pigs were eating, but no one gave him anything.[17]

"Because the young man found himself in a very difficult situation, he began to think about the meaning and purpose of his life. He used to have a great life on his father's ranch. He was required to work hard and be obedient to his father, but because he wanted to party with the devil, he took his inheritance and spent all his money on getting drunk; and now that he was totally broke and destitute, he found himself rolling around in the pig slop.

"In verse seventeen the Bible describes how the young man 'came to himself.'[18] What do you think that means? How does a person 'come to himself'? Other translations of the Bible say when he 'came to his senses.' When the young man came to his senses, he was probably wondering if it would be possible to bring the pig slop back into his father's house. Here he is getting drunk, doing drugs and screwing prostitutes—do you think it would be okay for him to bring all that filth back home into his father's house?"

At this point in the sermon, several homeless men got up to leave. Other men in the audience seemed agitated or distracted. A tall man seated in the front row said, "Pig slop will never be allowed in the father's house."

"Because the father in this story represents God, let me ask you another question," Matthew said. "Do you think the father is going to roll around in the pig slop with the son?"

Another man in the audience said, "Hell, no!"

"In order for the young man to 'come to his senses,' he had a choice to make," Matthew said. "Because it's not possible to bring pig slop into the father's house, he needed to leave it all behind. He needed to break all of his agreements with the devil, repent of his sins and return back to God.

"After the young man came to his senses, he said to himself, 'How many of my father's hired hands have bread enough and to spare, but here I am dying of hunger! I will get up and go to my father, and I will say to him, "Father, I have sinned against heaven and before you; I am no longer worthy to be called your son; treat me like one of your hired hands."'[19]

"The other problem this young man faced was that the longer he remained in the pigpen, the harder it would be for him to come to his senses. That's because when a man rolls around in the pig slop all day long, it hardens his heart. If the young man didn't have the strength to come to his senses today, what makes you think he will have the strength to do so next month, or even next year?"

Because nobody in the audience could answer the question, Matthew continued by saying, "As I was preparing this sermon, I began to wonder what would prevent a young man from coming to his senses. Do you think he was afraid of being rejected by his father?

"If we look at the father's love for the son, we can see that he wants him to come back home. Every day, the father walks down a long road to the edge of his property looking for his son, hoping that he will return.

"When the son decides to repent of his sins and return back to his father's house, we see the father's reaction in verse twenty-two, when he said to his servants, 'Quickly, bring out a robe—the best one—and put it on him; put a ring on his finger and sandals on his feet. And get the fatted calf and kill it, and let us eat and celebrate; for this son of mine was dead and is alive again; he was lost and is found!'[20]

"We have a loving God who wants each and every one of you to return back to his fellowship. Your situation is not hopeless. There's no reason to be afraid. God is not mad at you. God is not going to punish you. He's not going to reject you. If there's anyone in the audience who is tired of rolling around in the pig slop, who wants to enter into a good life on the father's ranch, we would like to pray with you. Please come to the front of the room. Everybody else is free to go downstairs to receive a hot meal."

After the missionaries spent over an hour ministering to seventeen men and two women who came forward for prayer, Michelle called a young lady over and said, "I would like to introduce you to Jacky."

"It's good to meet you," Matthew said. "I noticed you and Michelle talking in the back of the room."

"Jacky was sharing with me some of the difficulties that she has been experiencing," Michelle said. "She wanted us to pray with her, but after she told me about her involvement with the Wicca religion, I wanted to set up a time with you for a more in-depth conversation."

"I would be happy to meet with you," Matthew said. "I don't know much about the Wicca religion, except that practitioners cast spells utilizing the powers of earth, fire, water and wind."

"There are five basic elements," Jacky said. "Earth, fire, water, wind and spirit."

"I wanted to take Jacky to lunch at the Mongolian Fireside Grill next Friday after the service," Michelle said. "Would you be able to join us for a deeper conversation?"

"That would be great," Matthew said.

* * *

The Mongolian Fireside Grill was located about two miles from the Rescue Mission, so after the Friday afternoon service, Jacky and the missionaries were able to arrive at this popular lunch destination a little after one o'clock. Because the restaurant had an outdoor fenced-off seating section with tables and umbrellas on the southern side of the building, Michelle said, "Let's sit outside. It's such a nice day."

"That's fine by me," Jacky said as they entered the seating area. "I have never been here, but it sure does smell delicious."

"I love coming here," Michelle said. "It's buffet-style, so you fill a bowl with raw steak, chicken or shrimp. Then you add stir-fry vegetables and any other ingredients that will fit on top. Once your bowl is filled with everything you want in your stir-fry, you take it to a cooking station. The chefs will pour the contents of your bowl on a hot grill. You can also add nuts and a variety of sauces, or even an egg if you want it cooked into your dish."

After Jacky and the missionaries created their entrées and watched the chefs cook their creations on a hot grill, a waitress brought over a large bowl of rice and a plate of flour tortillas.

"Now you see why this is one of my favorite places to eat lunch," Michelle said, before she offered up a prayer to bless the food.

During the meal, Matthew started a conversation by saying, "I have never practiced the Wicca religion, so I went home and conducted some research on the Internet. I'm not sure if all my information is accurate, so please correct me if I say something that conflicts with your beliefs."

"I will let you know," Jacky said.

"From what I was able to discern, Wicca witchcraft starts with a request to enter into the spiritual realm," Matthew said. "Many of the spells contain different words, but the fundamental principles remain the same: The practitioner wants to access the sacred circle of spirits so that those spirits can interact with that person. The practitioner also wants to be united with those spirits in order to use their spiritual powers to get what they want.

"Once a practitioner enters into a spiritual circle and invites the power of the spirit guides into his or her life, that person will then utilize the elemental forces of earth, fire, water and wind to cast a spell in an attempt to bring about a desired result. Because earth is a physical element, it represents our source of food and shelter. It would also represent our physical bodies, strength and endurance.

"Because fire represents light and the sun, its flames contain destructive powers. Fire also represents our own personal power and assertiveness. Water represents life, because without water, there would be no life on earth. Water also represents purification, cleansing and rebirth. Wind represents the weather and is often associated with the sky and freedom. Wind also represents change, intuition and our ability to communicate.

"When a Wicca practitioner casts a spell, that person will enter into the sacred circle of spirits to unite himself or herself with those spiritual powers. Once they are united, the practitioner will combine those powers with earth, fire, water and wind—which also represent our own personal endurance, strength, assertiveness and the ability to communicate—in an attempt to bring about a desired result."

"That's an excellent description," Jacky said.

"From the Christian perspective, there are only three forces at work in the world," Matthew said. "On one side, we have God and his angelic army. At the opposite extreme, we have the devil or Satan and his vast army of fallen angels, known as demons. There's also the human dynamic, because God created us as spiritual beings with a soul.

"When a Wicca practitioner casts a spell by uniting himself or herself with those spiritual powers, that person thinks those powers are coming from God's creation of earth, fire, water and wind; but what would happen if those elements have no spiritual powers, and all the power is coming from demonic forces? What if when a Wicca practitioner casts a spell, that person is making an agreement with fallen angels in an attempt to utilize demonic powers?"

"That would explain all the strange phenomena that I have been experiencing," Jacky said. "When you were describing this to me, I could feel a strong sensation of anxiety coming over me. It feels like a panic attack that makes me want to get up and leave."

"Let's conduct a little experiment," Matthew said. "If my theory is correct, and you have opened yourself up to demonic forces, once they gain access to your life, they will not let you go without a fight. So with your permission, I would like to pray with you, asking God's angelic warriors to strike down and destroy anything evil or demonic that's interfering with you right now."

"You have my permission," Jacky said.

"Heavenly Father, we come before you sinful and in great need of your assistance," Matthew said. "Please build a spiritual canopy around us so that we can continue this conversation in peace. We ask this through our Lord Jesus Christ, through the power of the Holy Spirit, in Jesus' name we pray."

"That's so strange," Jacky said. "I feel different now."

"The concept for the spiritual canopy comes from the Book of Zechariah," Michelle said. "In the second chapter, the Lord promised to be a wall of fire around Jerusalem.[21] In the same way, we can ask the Lord to build a wall of fire around us, so that inside of this protective barrier, the Holy Spirit can dwell with us."

"In addition to the protective barrier," Matthew said, "I'm assuming that God's angelic warriors descended upon us and removed all the demonic spirits that were interfering with our conversation and causing your anxiety attacks. I'm not sure how long the protective barrier will last, but if you do not denounce all forms of witchcraft and enter into an authentic relationship with Jesus, the demonic spirits will most certainly return with a vengeance."

"I don't want that to happen," Jacky said.

"I would like to introduce Jacky to one of our women's Bible study groups," Michelle said. "I also think we should share the Gospel message with her and pray for her salvation."

After the missionaries continued ministering to Jacky for another hour, she was able to accept Jesus' sacrifice on the cross for the forgiveness of her sins. The heaviness that was constantly oppressing her spirit had been completely removed and replaced by tears of joy that were streaming down her face.

"If you will please excuse me," Jacky said. "I would like to visit the ladies' room."

After Jacky stepped away from the table, Matthew said, "You were right about an excellent source of ministry opportunities."

When Jacky returned to the table, she looked at Michelle and said, "I wanted to thank you for being such an inspiration to me."

"I'm the one who should be thanking you," Michelle said as she gave her friend a hug goodbye.

4th CHAPTER

When the missionaries returned to the Rescue Mission for the next chapel service, Matthew said to the audience, "I wanted to discuss all the deceptive ways the devil can use to creep into our lives. If you have a Bible, please turn with me to the eighteenth chapter of Deuteronomy.

"In verse ten, the Lord gives us specific instructions by saying, 'No one shall be found among you who makes a son or daughter pass through fire, or who practices divination, or is a soothsayer, or an augur, or a sorcerer, or one who casts spells, or who consults ghosts or spirits, or who seeks oracles from the dead. For whoever does these things is abhorrent to the Lord.'"[22]

After displaying an image of a Ouija board on the overhead projector, Matthew asked the audience, "Has anyone played with a Ouija board in the past?" Because several people in the audience raised their hands, Matthew continued his message by saying, "The Ouija board is not mentioned by name anywhere in the Bible, so many people may think that it's just a toy and that it's safe to use. In fact, it's possible to buy a Ouija board in many toy stores across America.

"If you are wondering how a Ouija board works, you simply take hold of the pointer and ask the spirit realm a question. Then you allow a spirit guide to move your hand around the board to spell out an answer.

"Now that we know how the Ouija board works, I would like to take a closer look at the Scripture passage from Deuteronomy to see if you can find where the Ouija board has been condemned by God, even though it's not specifically mentioned by name in the Bible."

After a long moment of silence, a man raised his hand and said, "Divination."

"Good answer," Matthew said. "Does anyone know what the word *divination* means? I looked it up in the dictionary, and it means 'acquiring information from supernatural sources.' When a person plays with the Ouija board, they are asking the spiritual realm a question. Just because a person doesn't receive an answer immediately, it doesn't mean that the spiritual entities will stop trying to interact with that person for the rest of his or her life.

"Let me give you an example of what that would look like in the spiritual realm. Let's say some teenage boys were playing with a Ouija board. In an attempt to acquire supernatural knowledge, they ask a spirit guide a question. If the spirit guide didn't move their hands around the board to spell out an answer, the boys might get frustrated and put the game back in the closet. Just because the boys put the game away doesn't mean that it's over. Ten years later, those same spiritual powers would still have the right to speak to those young men.

"Let's say one young man needed to make an important decision regarding his career path. God would want that young man to make the right choice, but the spiritual powers that operate behind the Ouija board would still have the right to influence that young man into making the wrong decision. If God's angels confronted those demonic spirits and asked them to leave the young man alone, they would refuse and respond by saying, 'He asked us to speak to him many years ago, and we are now delivering our answers.'

"The only way for the young man to permanently drive the demonic spirits out of his life would be to confess the sin of divination and denounce all forms of communication with those spiritual entities in the name, power and authority of Jesus. When we consider the fact that there are only three spiritual forces at work in the world, this scenario becomes even more disturbing.

"Because God's Word specifically tells us not to participate in the sin of divination, we know the spiritual powers behind the Ouija board are not coming from God. If the spiritual powers are not coming from God, where do you think they are coming from?"

"From the devil," a homeless man said.

"When those young men played with the Ouija board, they gave the devil and his vast army of fallen angels the right to influence their thoughts," Matthew said. "They gave deceptive spiritual entities the right to interact with them for the purpose of imparting hidden knowledge. We also know, from the tenth chapter of John's Gospel, that the devil and his vast army of fallen angels only have one purpose—to steal, kill and destroy.[23]

"If you have a history of making very bad decisions, you may want to take a look at the list of deadly agreements the devil can use to destroy our lives. Although the sin of fortune telling is not mentioned in the eighteenth chapter of Deuteronomy, it's still a form of divination.

"It doesn't matter if the fortune teller reads a crystal ball, uses tarot cards or studies the lines on your palm; when a person visits a fortune teller, those people are seeking information from supernatural sources.

"Because God's Word specifically condemns all forms of divination, including fortune telling, we know the information that the fortune teller provides is not coming from God. If the information is not coming from God, where do you think it's coming from?"

"It comes from the devil," another man called out.

"No, it doesn't!" another man said.

"The same is true for all other New Age and occult practices," Matthew said. "When a woman goes to the New Age bookstore and buys a book on spirit guide channeling, that woman is opening up her life, heart and soul to demonic spirits. It doesn't matter what form of spirit guide channeling the woman uses; it's all backed by the powers of the demonic.

"Some forms of channeling involve the use of crystals. Another form is called automatic writing. This process works when a practitioner asks demonic spirits to move his or her hand around to write messages on a piece of paper.

"Reiki energy healing is where people use Reiki power symbols to impart supernatural powers into other people's bodies for the purpose of so-called healing. In some forms of yoga, the participants will chant the names of demonic entities for the purpose of inviting spiritual powers into their bodies while exercising. Basically, all forms of witchcraft, including black and white magic, Santeria and voodoo, all involve demonic powers that are sent forth to bring about a desired result.

"If there's anyone in the audience who has ever participated in any kind of New Age or occult activity, I would like to say a two-part prayer with you. In the first part of the prayer, it's important to acknowledge the New Age or occult activity as sinful, and after you acknowledge why it's wrong, you can confess your sins to Jesus and ask for his forgiveness.

"In the second part of the prayer, you will need to break all agreements with the demonic spirits and drive them out of your life in the name, power and authority of Jesus. So let's take a moment to examine our conscience and invite the Holy Spirit into our lives to bring up any events from your past when you made an agreement with demonic spirits, so that you can be set free."

At the end of the service, when Matthew was escorting Michelle to her Jeep, she said, "That was another excellent message. I could feel a lot of darkness and depression lifting off of those guys when they were commanding the demonic spirits to flee."

"Thanks for the encouragement," Matthew said. "I wanted to invite you on a date this weekend."

"What did you have in mind?" Michelle asked.

"I would like to spend the weekend with you at the beach on a Caribbean island," Matthew said, "but because I don't have a job and need to save money to pay my rent next month, I was thinking about a free day at the zoo."

"That sounds wonderful," Michelle said.

"I also wanted to test our new African backpacking stove," Matthew said. "So for lunch, I was thinking about organic chicken tenders that have been sautéed in garlic and smothered with olive oil and sesame seeds. I was planning to cook the chicken tenders at my house, so all we need to do is warm them up in the back of my 4Runner for lunch.

"I was hoping you could bring two frying pans so that we could heat the pita bread in one pan, and warm up the chicken tenders with shredded provolone cheese in the other pan. I will also bring some black olives, red onion and yellow bell peppers."

"That sounds delicious," Michelle said.

* * *

The Woodland Park Zoo was located near the art

museum in the historical district. It was surrounded by older brick buildings on the southern side and the Grand Central Golf Course on the northern side.

When the missionaries arrived early Saturday morning, Matthew parked his 4Runner at the end of the lot near an irrigation canal under the shade of a tall maple tree. That way he could prepare lunch away from the crowds of people who normally visit the zoo on the weekends.

"Do you want to stop by the visitor center to get a map?" Matthew asked as they approached the entrance.

"Let's just go exploring today," Michelle said. "I have been praying to be more in tune with the Holy Spirit's guidance. I want to flow with God's Spirit as he leads and guides me through life, so that I'm not rushing ahead or falling behind, but maintaining perfect harmony at all times."

"I need to be more sensitive in that area," Matthew said. "It seems like every time I get in trouble, I'm rushing around out of alignment, so today would be the perfect opportunity for me to practice my sensitivity and obedience to the Holy Spirit's guidance."

"I have also been praying about some fundraising opportunities," Michelle said as they approached an exhibit that contained giraffes, zebras and wildebeests.

"I like how they have mixed all these animals together in the same enclosure," Matthew said. "This is exactly what we would experience in the African wilderness, except there wouldn't be any fences and the boundaries would be much larger."

"I'm sure there would also be hungry lions hiding in the bushes," Michelle said. "That way the herd animals wouldn't look so bored, standing around all day as they wait for their next meal."

"That would certainly create some excitement," Matthew said.

As the missionaries watched how the giraffes were interacting with the zebras, Michelle said, "Last week I noticed a homeless man standing on the corner. He was holding a cardboard sign that said, 'Will Work for Food.' The sign he was holding looked very old. It was weathered and tattered on the edges, as if he had used it for many years. I was thinking about rolling down my window and offering him a few dollars to buy that sign."

"Why would you want his sign?" Matthew asked.

"If we could gather a collection of the most interesting and creative homeless signs, we could ask Monica to put them on display in her art gallery," Michelle said. "We would need about two hundred signs to fill the upper and lower levels; but if Monica would agree, we could invite all our sponsors and Jclub members for a homeless fundraising event."

"That's a great idea," Matthew said. "Do you think Monica would want to display homeless signs in her prestigious gallery?"

"She knows a lot of wealthy people," Michelle said. "If we offer her a twenty percent commission, she would probably even help us advertise."

"I'm wondering how hard it would be to acquire that many signs," Matthew said.

"It would probably take us several months," Michelle said. "Let's start small and buy three or four signs next week. Then I could show the samples to Monica to see what she says. If she doesn't like the idea, we could always rent another gallery or host our homeless sign exhibit somewhere else."

"I like the idea because it will empower the homeless," Matthew said. "Instead of standing on the street corner begging for money, a homeless man would be empowered to act like an entrepreneur. If the homeless man sells his cardboard sign for two dollars, that person would need to make another sign; and in doing so, he would be creating a product in exchange for the money. That person would also need to negotiate a business transaction to receive the money."

"If a homeless man has a really nice sign, maybe we could start the conversation by offering him two dollars and then work our way up to five dollars," Michelle said.

"I have also been thinking about a homeless trash pickup project where we pay a homeless person to clean up all the trash around the Rescue Mission," Matthew said. "That way, they would be able to earn money by offering a valuable service to society."

After exploring the sea lion exhibit, the missionaries visited the aviary, which consisted of a series of greenhouse-styled buildings with thirty-foot-tall glass ceilings.

"Check out that squirrel over there," Matthew said.

"Do you think he slipped in here to eat the bird's food, or do you think he's part of the exhibit?"

"I'm not sure," Michelle said. "Although he's very adorable, I like the flamingos, penguins and swans the best."

"I also wanted to address some of your Catholic Church concerns," Matthew said. "I thought we could start with some simple topics and work our way up to the more complex theological issues."

"This ought to be interesting," Michelle said.

"To understand the Catholic Church, it's important that we go back in time to study church history," Matthew said. "When I looked up the word *Catholic* in the dictionary, it means the 'original' Christian Church that existed before the Protestant Reformation. The definition also includes the term 'universal,' so to be Catholic means to be part of the universal Christian Church that existed before the Protestant Reformation.[24]

"I also researched the Southern Baptist Church, which was founded in 1845. After the Protestant Reformation occurred in the fifteenth century, a pastor from Amsterdam rejected the concept of infant baptism and established a new religion where only adult believers could be baptized by water immersion.

"After his church members, who were called Baptists, migrated to America, a dispute broke out between the Northern Baptists and the Southern Baptists over slavery. Apparently, the Southern Baptists were using God's Word to justify and defend slavery, while the

Northern Baptists argued that the Christian laws of love would prevent a person from owning another human being as a piece of property."

"Let's visit the panda exhibit next," Michelle said.

"Sixteen years after the Southern Baptist Church parted ways with the Northern Baptists, a civil war broke out in America. After the civil war ended, Congress abolished slavery by ratifying the thirteenth amendment of the Constitution, which says that neither slavery nor involuntary servitude shall exist within the United States. Since that time, the leadership of the Southern Baptist Church has not only apologized for owning slaves in the past, but they also apologized for using Christian ideology to defend slavery."

"What does this have to do with chanting hail Mary prayers to an assortment of statues over and over again?" Michelle asked.

"I'm just establishing the importance of going back in time to study church history," Matthew said.

"History was one of my favorite subjects in school," Michelle said.

"Then let's go back to the first century to see what happened after the Book of Acts was written," Matthew said. "In Saint Paul's letter to Titus, he said, 'I left you behind in Crete for this reason, so that you should put in order what remained to be done, and should appoint elders in every town, as I directed you.'[25]

"According to Saint Paul's instructions, whenever a new church was planted, in every town or region, an overseer was appointed. These men were part of the first-century Christian church, and they were held accountable to the Apostles in Jerusalem.

"We can also see from Sacred Scripture that Peter was the leader of the Apostles, because Christ gave him the keys of the kingdom of heaven when he said, 'You are Peter, and on this rock I will build my church, and the gates of Hades will not prevail against it. I will give you the keys of the kingdom of heaven, and whatever you bind on earth will be bound in heaven, and whatever you loose on earth will be loosed in heaven.'[26]

"We can also see from church history that when Peter died, another overseer was appointed to take his place. The names of Peter's successors have been recorded in history as Linus, Cletus and Clement. After Saint Clement died, there was an unbroken succession of Popes from Peter to our present-day Bishop of Rome. We can also see from Sacred Scripture that Saint Paul was obedient to the Church's leadership structure.

"For example, when an argument broke out in the Book of Acts regarding circumcision, Paul and Barnabas were appointed to go up to Jerusalem to discuss the situation with the Apostles.[27] When Paul and Barnabas arrived, the Apostles and elders welcomed them, and they reported all that God had done through them.

"After the Apostles and elders met together to discuss the matter of circumcision, they chose men from among their ranks and sent them to Antioch along with a letter that said, 'It has seemed good to the Holy Spirit and to us to impose on you no further burden than these essentials: that you abstain from what has been sacrificed to idols and from blood and from what is strangled and from fornication.'[28]

"So we can see from the Bible that the first-century Christian church had a hierarchy of leadership; and in every town where a church was established, a Bishop was appointed as an overseer for that region. Whenever a Bishop had a theological concern, he would bring that issue to the Apostles so that the problem could be addressed and resolved.

"As the Church continued to grow, the devil and his vast army of fallen angels tried to influence the diverse religious communities with false doctrines, secret knowledge, gnosticism, superstition and all kinds of lies about the divinity of Christ. For example, was Jesus fully divine and devoid of all human nature, or was he fully human and devoid of all divinity?

"All these issues needed to be resolved by the leaders of the Church, so in the third century, all the Bishops from every region in the world met together in modern-day Turkey in a town called Nicaea to establish the Nicene Creed, which says, 'We believe in one God, the Father Almighty, maker of heaven and earth, of all things visible and invisible. We believe in one Lord Jesus Christ, the only begotten Son of God, born of the Father before all ages. God from God, Light from Light, true God from true God, begotten, not made, consubstantial with the Father; through him all things were made...'[29]

"During the third-century meeting in Nicaea, they called the Bishops who established our modern-day concept of the Trinity, *Doctors of the Church*. They also referred to these men as our early *Church Fathers*. If you search the Internet for the term 'Church Fathers,' you will find Saint Jerome, Saint Augustine and Saint Ambrose. The word *saint* just means a person who has been sanctified by the blood of Christ and set apart for God.

"Saint Paul also referred to himself as a spiritual 'father' in his First Letter to the Corinthians, when he said, 'Though you might have ten thousand guardians in Christ, you do not have many fathers. Indeed, in Christ Jesus I became your father through the Gospel. I appeal to you, then, be imitators of me. For this reason I sent you Timothy, who is my beloved and faithful child in the Lord.'"[30]

"In the Gospel of Matthew, Jesus says, 'Call no one your father on earth, for you have one Father—the one in heaven,'"[31] Michelle said.

"I know, and we will get to that passage in a minute," Matthew said, "but think about what you are implying. Saint Paul calls himself a spiritual father, and he addresses Timothy in his letter as 'My loyal child in the faith.'[32]

"Are you saying that Saint Paul is deceived? Are you saying the guy who wrote the majority of the New Testament doesn't know what he is talking about, and that we need to remove his letters to Timothy from the

Bible and revise his letters to the Corinthians?"

"I acknowledge the entire Bible as the authoritative Word of God," Michelle said.

"I know you do," Matthew said. "That's why I spent a lot of time researching this topic, and I don't want our conversation to get disrespectful. So far, I have explained to you why Catholics refer to their parish priests as spiritual fathers. The tradition started when Saint Paul referred to himself as a spiritual father and referred to Timothy as his spiritual child in the Lord.

"The Bible also says, 'Let the elders who rule well be considered worthy of double honor, especially those who labor in preaching and teaching.'[33] So in an attempt to honor preachers and teachers, Catholics have been calling those who serve well their spiritual fathers for thousands of years."

"What about the Lord's command in the Gospel of Matthew?" Michelle asked.

"Let's look at the words of Christ in the twenty-third chapter," Matthew said. "In the entire section, Jesus is condemning the Pharisees. In that specific verse, he said, 'Call no one your father on earth, for you have one Father—the one in heaven. Nor are you to be called instructors, for you have one instructor, the Messiah. The greatest among you will be your servant. All who exalt themselves will be humbled, and all who humble themselves will be exalted.'[34]

"Because the Lord concludes his teaching with a warning for those who exalt themselves, I think the deeper meaning of this passage is to be on guard against all forms of spiritual pride."

"Would that include contributing to the sin of spiritual pride in the lives of preachers and teachers by the way we address them?" Michelle asked.

"Let's look at our options," Matthew said. "If you don't like addressing Father O'Connor as a spiritual father, then you could call him Pastor O'Connor or Reverend O'Connor. Apparently, it's okay to call an overseer a Bishop or address him as Most Reverend, but in some Dioceses, I have heard Catholics refer to their Bishops as Most Holy Excellency."

"Something doesn't feel right about calling a sinful man your Most Holy Excellency," Michelle said. "Jesus died a very painful death on the cross to pay the penalty for our sins so that we could enter into an authentic relationship with our Heavenly Father. He even went so far as to call our Heavenly Father 'Abba' or daddy.

"He also doesn't want us to call anyone our spiritual instructors or spiritual directors, because Jesus wants to be our only source for spiritual direction. The entire purpose of the Christian walk is to enter into an authentic relationship with the Blessed Trinity, but that's not going to be possible when we allow sinful men to take that place in our lives and hearts."

"I couldn't agree with you more," Matthew said.

"Thank you," Michelle said.

"Do you want to stop for lunch now?" Matthew asked.

"I'm starting to get a little hungry," Michelle said, "but it doesn't feel like we have resolved anything. There has to be a better way to attribute honor to those who serve well than to inflate their egos with spiritual pride."

As the missionaries were walking back to the parking lot to warm up the pita bread sandwiches on their new camping stove, Michelle stopped in front of an exhibit and said, "How adorable! Look at all those playful lemurs."

"They have beautiful golden eyes," Matthew said.

"I wonder if they would make good house pets," Michelle said as she removed her phone from her purse to search the Internet. "They have soft fur like a house cat, climb around like little monkeys and have black and white stripes like a raccoon. What a perfect combination of fun."

"What did you discover?" Matthew asked.

"One source said that lemurs are wild animals and could not be domesticated," Michelle said. "Another website said lemurs could not be potty trained, and that they need socialization with other lemurs. They will also bite and scratch humans."

"That doesn't sound like a very good house pet," Matthew said. "Besides, they would probably wreak havoc on your mom's curtains and lighting fixtures."

"I was thinking we could get two lemurs, a baby boy and a little girl, and let them grow up in your apartment," Michelle said.

"I have a better idea that comes with a surprise," Matthew said. "How about we spend the evening in prayer about our conversation today, and then we can continue it tomorrow afternoon at Greenwood Village Park?"

"What kind of surprise were you thinking about?" Michelle asked.

5th CHAPTER

Greenwood Village Park had a reputation for being a romantic rendezvous for young couples. The main attraction was a series of man-made lakes and small islands that were connected together by arching bridges. The outer perimeter of the park consisted of tall trees and flower beds with bright green fern bushes and yellow flowers. The cobblestone walkways that wove throughout the park were illuminated with Victorian-style streetlights, and their matching park benches were located nearby.

When the missionaries arrived, Michelle said, "The water is so calm, you can see a perfect reflection of the sky, trees and bridges; and here come some ducks."

After opening his backpack, Matthew said, "For your first surprise, I stopped by the store this morning and bought two loaves of bread."

As soon as Michelle started tearing off small pieces of bread and throwing them in the water, more ducks started coming. It didn't take long before a small flock

of water fowl started competing with each other over every piece of bread that landed in the water.

Because the ducks were starting to make a disturbance, Matthew put the remaining bread back in his backpack and started walking toward the boat dock.

When the missionaries reached the other side of the lake, Michelle looked back and said, "That duck is following us. He's paddling so hard you can see a V-shaped wake in the water. Can we please give him some more bread?"

"I should have bought three loaves," Matthew said

as he handed Michelle the half-empty bag.

After Michelle fed the duck another piece of bread, Matthew said, "After praying about our conversation last night, I wanted to acknowledge that you're right. There's a problem in the Catholic Church with some parishioners who have turned their spiritual director into a false god. I have met many Catholics who are deeply devoted to their religious practices but are devoid of an authentic relationship with Jesus.

"For example, when I asked Deacon Bill if he wanted to go on a mission trip with us, he started making all kinds of excuses. Instead of taking the opportunity to his Lord and Master in prayer, he wanted to ask his wife and his spiritual director for permission. Even if his spiritual director thought it would be a good idea to fulfill the Great Commission, I'm sure his wife would find all kinds of objections.

"Other Catholics I have met think that if they do whatever the parish priest tells them, it will somehow make them okay with God. It's almost like they have a subconscious desire to replace an authentic relationship with God with their parish priest."

"I thought there was a famous Catholic theologian who said, 'Thou hast made us for thyself, O Lord, and our heart is restless until it finds its rest in thee,'" Michelle said. "It's almost like we have a God-shaped vacuum deep within our hearts, and we try to fill that void with anything other than the one true God."

"Jesus wants to be the Lord of our lives; but instead

of making Jesus the Lord of our lives, we turn to religion and end up making a parish priest our god, or the Catholic Church our god, or a Christian counselor our god, or even a spiritual director our god," Matthew said.

"As missionaries for Christ, it's our job to make sure everybody has entered into an authentic relationship with the Blessed Trinity," Michelle said.

"Which brings us to our next conversation about infant baptism," Matthew said, "but first, I wanted to present your second surprise."

As the missionaries walked down a cobblestone path, they approached a set of concrete stairs that were covered in moss. At the bottom landing, there was a wooden deck along with a fleet of blue-and-white-colored rowboats.

"Are we going on a boat ride?" Michelle asked with excitement.

"The rental shack is right over there," Matthew said.

After renting a rowboat for three hours, Michelle sat in front as Matthew gave her a tour of the islands, bridges and waterways. Halfway through the tour, Matthew said, "To understand infant baptism, it will be helpful to discuss the steps necessary for salvation.

"For Catholics, salvation is a past, present and future event, similar to a marriage. For example, at some point in a married couple's past, they exchanged wedding vows; after that point, they would consider themselves to be married. In the same way, a non-believer can make a commitment to serve Christ; and afterward, that person would consider himself or herself to be saved.

"Salvation is also a present-day event, because like a marriage, our relationship with God requires our full devotion. If I neglect and abuse my wife, my marriage will end in divorce. If I abuse, neglect and denounce my relationship with Christ, my salvation will also end in divorce. That's because salvation is also a future event. If obtaining salvation means avoiding eternal condemnation and entering into our eternal heavenly home, then nobody on earth has actually been saved yet, until that person passes through the final judgment and enters into his or her heavenly home.

"The Bible also speaks about salvation as a past, present and future event. For example, in Saint Paul's letter to the Romans he says, 'For in hope we were saved.'[35] He is speaking in the past tense and referring to a point in a person's past when that person accepted the Gospel message and made a commitment to follow Christ.

"In Saint Paul's letter to the Philippians, he was speaking in the present tense when he said, 'Work out your own salvation with fear and trembling.'[36] When Saint Paul wrote this letter to the church in Philippi, he was instructing the Christian believers in Philippi to constantly maintain their relationship with Jesus, because an authentic relationship with Jesus will cost a person everything.

"Jesus also gave us many parables about counting the cost of discipleship. For example, in the Gospel of

Luke, Jesus says, 'Whoever does not carry the cross and follow me cannot be my disciple.'[37] He then continued this teaching by describing a person who began to build a tower that could not be finished. The work of carrying our cross and building the tower needs to be accomplished in the present.

"Salvation is also a future event, because in the Gospel of Matthew, Jesus says only those who endure to the end will be saved.[38] Saint Paul makes the same point in his letter to the Corinthians when he wrote about being disqualified from entering into his heavenly home after spending so much time preaching the Gospel message to others. He was so concerned about being disqualified that he punished and enslaved his own body, so that after proclaiming the Good News of salvation to other people, he might not be disqualified.[39]

"At the opposite extreme, there are many mainstream Christian churches that believe in 'once-saved, always-saved.' They teach that once a person accepts Jesus as their personal Lord and Savior, they are guaranteed to go to heaven. I'm not sure what Bible verse they use to justify this teaching, but they will say that Jesus will do everything necessary to make sure that person enters into their heavenly home."

"I have a theory on why so many mainstream churches preach messages that affirm a person's salvation," Michelle said. "There was a large Christian book publishing company many years ago that spent millions of dollars conducting a survey in an attempt to find out what message their book-reading audience wanted to hear the most. They wanted to know what message would make a best-selling book, what message would make the most popular Christian song, or what message would make a great sermon. You will never guess what they discovered?"

"Please, tell me," Matthew said.

"The most desired message that mainstream Christians want to hear is the assurance of their own salvation," Michelle said. "This survey makes a lot of sense when you study the lyrics of the number-one Christian songs, or common themes from our most popular television evangelists. Mainstream Christians want to know that their sins have been forgiven and that they are guaranteed to enter heaven. They also want to know that nothing can separate them from God's love. This psychological drive is so great that many people will seek out any preachers, teachers, radio show hosts or television evangelists who will tell them what they want to hear."

"I met a homeless man last week who told me the same thing," Matthew said. "The guy was getting drunk in the bushes in the park down the street from the Rescue Mission. When I asked him if he was a Christian, he assured me that he was saved and that nothing could separate him from God's love.

"After thinking about what this man said, the first thought that came to my mind was hardness of heart. Would a constant state of sin and disobedience prevent this man from accomplishing God's will in his life?"

"There's a passage from the Book of Hebrews that I want to look up," Michelle said as she searched the application on her phone. "'For if we willfully persist in sin after having received the knowledge of the truth, there no longer remains a sacrifice for sins, but a fearful prospect of judgment.'"[40]

"There was a Christian author many years ago who wrote a best-selling book on dating," Matthew said. "I'm not sure of all the details, but when he was a youth pastor, his book became a bestseller, so the elders at his church made him the senior pastor. Not long after, he married a woman who worked at the church; then several years later, the couple announced they were getting divorced.

"After his divorce, the man made public statements explaining why he was 'taking a break from Christianity' and apologized for the Christian content in his book. He also demanded that the publisher remove his book from the market as he stepped down from the leadership role at the church.

"After doing everything possible to denounce Christianity, he reappeared several years later on social media at a gay pride parade. He was taking photographs with his male friends, wearing LGBT apparel and eating cupcakes with rainbow-colored frosting. In this man's situation, would you say that because he was once-saved he is always-saved and guaranteed to go to heaven?"

"I don't know what is going to happen to him on

the Day of Judgment," Michelle said.

"That's exactly the answer I wanted to hear," Matthew said. "If I were God, I could assure this man's salvation; or if I were God, I could also assure this man's eternal damnation; but because I'm not God, it's not my decision to make! And if it's not my decision to make, how can any reputable Christian pastor, radio show host or television evangelist assure anyone's salvation or eternal damnation?"

"In the Sermon on the Mount, Jesus describes the road that leads to everlasting life as hard and narrow, and there are few people who find it,"[41] Michelle said. "The man who is taking a break from Christianity is either traveling the hard and narrow road that leads to everlasting life, or he has taken a detour by embracing the wide and easy road that leads to eternal damnation."

"Now that we have established that salvation is referred to as a past, present and future event in the Bible, let's look at infant baptism," Matthew said. "The Catholic Church teaches that baptism is necessary for salvation. This doctrine is based on the Gospel of John when Jesus said to Nicodemus, 'No one can enter the kingdom of God without being born of water and Spirit.'[42] Saint Paul makes the same point in his letter to Titus, when he says that we are not saved by any works of righteousness, but 'through the water of rebirth and renewal by the Holy Spirit.'[43]

"The Catholic Church also teaches that adult baptism purifies a person of all their past sins, makes that person a new creature in Christ, and prepares that person's heart to become a temple of the Holy Spirit.[44] In the case of infant baptism, it removes the effects of original sin, consecrates a person for Christian worship, and imparts an indelible spiritual mark on a person's soul that can never be removed.[45]

"I realize all this sounds very deep and complex, but allow me to break it down for you in simpler terms. First of all, let me say that just because the Catholic Church considers baptism an important part of the salvation process, this Sacrament by itself doesn't guarantee any-body's salvation.

"Just because a person is baptized, it doesn't mean that person is guaranteed to go to heaven. The Catholic Church makes it very clear that a person's faith needs to grow after baptism.[46] So to understand why the Catholic Church baptizes infants, we have to go back to the first-century Christian church.

"In the Book of Acts, after Peter preached a power-ful sermon to a large audience, the Bible says that the men were cut to the heart and said to Peter, 'What should we do?'[47] Peter responds to their question by saying, 'Repent, and be baptized every one of you in the name of Jesus Christ so that your sins may be forgiven; and you will receive the gift of the Holy Spirit. For the promise is for you, for your children, and for all who are far away.'[48]

"Keep in mind that there was no day care in the first-century Christian church. In this large audience, where over three thousand people were baptized in one day, there were many mothers with small children. Peter just said to a large gathering of people that the New Covenant was open to everybody, including their children. We also need to keep in mind that Jews were accustomed to allowing their male children to enter the Old Covenant when they were eight days old.

"For example, when John the Baptist was eight days old, his parents took him to the temple to be circumcised.[49] This practice was established by God in the Book of Genesis when the Lord said to Abraham, 'This is my covenant, which you shall keep, between me and you and your offspring after you: Every male among you shall be circumcised. Throughout your generations every male among you shall be circumcised when he is eight days old.'[50]

"So you have a large crowd of Jewish families that consisted of men, women and children. The Jews had already been commanded by God to circumcise their children on the eighth day of their birth so they could enter into the Old Covenant. So when Peter said the promise of the New Covenant was for everybody, including their children, it would have been very natural for Jewish mothers to want their children to be baptized.

"If there were any theological issues with the first-century Christian church baptizing children, there would have been a big dispute as well as a teaching about infant baptism recorded in Sacred Scripture. Peter would have raised an objection by saying the promise is for everybody except small children, because they need to be of the age of reason before they can be baptized.

"Instead of seeing an objection to infant baptism, we see the exact opposite. When Lydia accepted the Gospel message in the Book of Acts, the Bible says her entire household was baptized.[51] When the jailer accepted the Gospel message, the Bible says his entire family was baptized without delay.[52] In Paul's letter to the Colossians, he compares baptism to circumcision by saying that we were 'circumcised with a spiritual circumcision' when we were 'buried with him in baptism.'[53]

"So to answer the age-old question of why the Catholic Church baptizes infants, we have been doing so since the Day of Pentecost and have a history of baptizing infants for over two thousand years. So let me ask you a question: Why wouldn't you want your baby baptized into the Christian faith?"

"I would," Michelle said.

"I realize we haven't had the opportunity to talk about having children together, but if we did, I would want my baby to be baptized by someone who believes in the ability to impart the indelible seed of the Holy Spirit into a child's life. If you don't think Clergyman O'Connor is the right person for this task, I'm sure we could find someone else."

"The problem with infant baptism is that a newborn baby is not old enough to choose Jesus as his or her personal Lord and Savior," Michelle said.

"Although that's true," Matthew said, "keep in

mind that if God allowed infants to enter the Old Covenant when they were eight days old, he will also allow infants to enter the New Covenant when they are eight days old; that's because the New Covenant is based on grace. In addition, God has given parents a certain amount of spiritual authority over their children. For example, during an infant baptism, parents dedicate their child to God in the same way Hannah dedicated the Prophet Samuel to God.[54]

"As the waters of baptism flow over the child's head, the parents would be laying hands on their baby while praying, 'O God, we give this child to you. We dedicate our baby to you. We ask you to impart the gifts of the Holy Spirit into our child's life in the same way that John the Baptist was filled with the Holy Spirit when he was still inside his mother's womb.'"[55]

"I have heard stories of Satanists who have dedicated their children to the devil," Michelle said. "In one situation, the couple needed to take their baby to an exorcist priest because he was speaking profanities in a man's voice."

"That's a good point," Matthew said. "If God would allow Satanists to dedicate their children to the devil, and if demonic spirits were allowed to enter into that child's life and speak profanities through the child using a man's voice, then God would also allow Christian parents to dedicate their children to the Blessed Trinity so that those children could receive the gift of the Holy Spirit."

"What is the indelible seed that you were talking about?" Michelle asked. "I'm assuming the word *indelible* means that it's permanent and cannot be erased."

"I'm sure the Catholic Church has an entire teaching about this in the *Catechism* that explains this concept in greater detail," Matthew said.[56] "From my experience, I was baptized when I was fourteen days old. When I was a little boy, long before I reached the age of reason where I could accept Jesus as my personal Lord and Savior, I could feel the Holy Spirit working in my life.

"I remember the first time I stole a piece of candy from the drugstore. Even though I never got caught, the Holy Spirit was all over me. I knew it was wrong because the Holy Spirit was alive and active in my life, convicting me of sin long before I accepted the Gospel message. I believe the Holy Spirit was allowed to operate in my life because I received the indelible seed of the Holy Spirit when my parents baptized me as an infant.

"Once an infant is baptized in the Catholic Church, the parents and godparents are required to teach their children about the Christian faith.[57] In my situation, my parents sent me to a Catholic grade school where the religious sisters taught us about Jesus. The Catholic Church also has another Sacrament called *Confirmation*. During Confirmation, a child who has reached the age of reason will acknowledge Jesus as his or her personal Lord and Savior; and afterward, that person is once again filled with the Holy Spirit through the anointing of chrism oil and the laying on of hands by a Bishop."

"Is that what happened to you?" Michelle asked.

"I had a messed-up childhood," Matthew said. "During my Confirmation, I was more concerned about this goofy polyester suit that my mother made me wear than I was about receiving the power of the Holy Spirit. Although my life is a poor example of the infilling of the Holy Spirit that occurs during Confirmation, I know without a shadow of a doubt that I received the Holy Spirit when I was baptized as an infant."

"If the Catholic Church can impart the gift of the Holy Spirit to infants during baptism, that would be so much better than allowing a child to go through all those years of life unprotected," Michelle said. "Especially when you consider how hostile our public schools have become with their LGBT agendas, drag queen story hours and gender-free bathrooms. I can't imagine all the confusion elementary school children must face growing up in today's negative and hostile environment."

"I would definitely want my children to receive the inner power and protection of the Holy Spirit while they were still inside their mother's womb," Matthew said. "Then immediately after they were born, I would have my children baptized so that little boy or girl could receive the indelible spiritual mark of the Holy Spirit and be sealed for the Day of Redemption.

"I would also read Bible stories to my children every evening before they went to sleep. As soon as they reached the age of reason, I would present the Gospel

message to them so they could make their own decision to follow Christ and accomplish God's will in their
lives."

"That sounds like a beautiful plan," Michelle said as
the rowboat passed underneath a bridge that connected
two islands together. "Can we come back here another
day to discuss why Catholics have to confess their sins to
a man in a dark room instead of going directly to God?"

"I will work on that presentation next week,"
Matthew said, "right after I prepare a message for the
homeless regarding the assurance of their salvation."

6th CHAPTER

When the missionaries arrived at the Rescue Mission for the next chapel service, Matthew began praying for the audience's ability to hear and receive the message with open minds and hearts, while Michelle greeted the guests at the door, making sure everybody felt welcome.

When the room filled to capacity, Michelle shut the exterior doors as Matthew walked up on stage, took hold of the microphone and said, "Please turn with me to the Second Letter of Paul to the Corinthians. In the thirteenth chapter, Saint Paul says, 'Examine yourselves to see whether you are living in the faith. Test yourselves. Do you not realize that Jesus Christ is in you? Unless, indeed, you fail to meet the test!'[58]

"In this passage, Saint Paul is addressing the Christian church in Corinth. He is writing to a group of Christians who have accepted Jesus as their personal Lord and Savior, yet he is asking them to examine themselves to make sure they are truly saved. If everybody from the church in Corinth was truly saved and guaranteed to go to heaven, why would Saint Paul be asking them to examine themselves?"

Because nobody in the audience could answer that question, Matthew went on to say, "Please turn with me to the Book of Revelation. In the second chapter, the Apostle John warns the church in Ephesus about abandoning their true love for Jesus. He said to them, 'I have this against you, that you have abandoned the love you had at first. Remember then from what you have fallen; repent, and do the works you did at first. If not, I will come to you and remove your lampstand from its place.'[59]

"We know from chapter one that the seven lamp-stands represent the seven churches.[60] So if this church doesn't repent and change its ways, Jesus will come and enforce a form of punishment on these believers by removing their lampstand from its place.

"There was also a church in Sardis that received a similar warning. In chapter three, the Apostle John says, 'I know your works; you have a name of being alive, but you are dead. Wake up, and strengthen what remains and is on the point of death, for I have not found your works perfect in the sight of my God. Remember then what you received and heard; obey it, and repent. If you do not wake up, I will come like a thief, and you will not know at what hour I will come.'[61]

"We also have a community of believers who gather together at the Rescue Mission. After studying these Scripture passages, I'm wondering if the same message that applied to the churches in Corinth, Ephesus and Sardis would also apply to this community. What do you think? Is everybody in this room saved and guaranteed to go to heaven? Or do you think some of us have back-slidden and fallen away from an authentic relationship with our Lord and Savior, Jesus Christ?"

"There's no such thing as God!" a drunken man yelled out from the back of the room.

"That's an interesting perspective," Matthew said. "I would like to know how many people in the audience consider themselves to be Christian by the show of hands. If you consider yourself to be Charismatic, Pentecostal, Evangelical, Church of Christ, Presbyterian, Seventh-Day Adventist, Methodist, Lutheran, Orthodox, Catholic or Baptist, please raise your hand."

Because one-third of the audience raised their hands, Matthew said, "I'm wondering how many people would consider themselves to be atheist or agnostic. If you don't know what those terms mean, an *atheist* doesn't believe in God's existence; an *agnostic* doesn't know what to believe about God because that person has never had an encounter with God."

Because a large number of people in the audience raised their hands, Matthew said, "I have another presentation that I would like to share with you next week that proves God's existence, but today, I would like to share with you a powerful self-examination test. The test is designed to see if you are an authentic Christian or if you have been deceived.

"It doesn't matter to me what Christian denomination you are from, because from God's perspective, we are called to be one body. Sacred Scripture says that there shall be 'no divisions' among us.[62] That's because from God's perspective, there are only two classifications of people: You are either a sheep or a goat, weeds or wheat. You are either a child of God or a child of the devil.[63]

"The self-examination test is important because most people in the world today think they are saved and guaranteed to go to heaven. I'm sure if we conducted a survey inside every church in America, the majority of people would think they were saved and guaranteed to go to heaven, but if we applied the self-examination test to their lives, I'm wondering if the majority of those people could pass the test.

"The self-examination test is easy to use and apply to our lives, because all you need to do is read the First Letter of John, meditate on the content and evaluate the meaning for your life. Let me give you an example of how this works. In chapter five, the Apostle John says, 'Those who believe in the Son of God have the testimony in their hearts.'[64]

"The only way you are going to get the testimony of Jesus in your heart is by inviting the presence of Jesus to dwell in your heart. To see if you can pass this test, all you need to do is ask yourself if there was ever a point in your past when you invited the presence of Jesus into your life and heart.

"In chapter four, the Apostle John says, 'By this we know that we abide in him and he in us, because he has given us of his Spirit.'[65] Was there ever a point in your past when you received the infilling of the Holy Spirit? In chapter two, the Apostle John says, 'By this we may be sure that we know him, if we obey his commandments. Whoever says, "I have come to know him," but does not obey his commandments, is a liar, and in such a person the truth does not exist.'"[66]

"You're the one who's telling lies," another drunk man screamed out from the back of the room. "The Bible says we are saved by faith and not by works."

"That's another very interesting perspective," Matthew said. "Let me ask you a question about the devil's faith. We know from Sacred Scripture that the devil believes in God. The Bible says that the demons believe in God and shudder.[67] We also know that Lucifer spent a lot of time in heaven before he was stripped of his power and cast down to earth. So what's the difference between the devil's faith in God and your faith in God?"

Because many people in the audience started laughing at the man who made the comment, Matthew said, "Think about that for a second. The devil knows that Jesus died on the cross to pay the penalty for our sins. The devil stirred up an angry crowd and watched Jesus suffer in agony on the cross, but no one in this room was there.

"The devil has spent a lot of time with God in

heaven, but no one in this room has ever taken a tour of heaven. I'm sure the devil could memorize the entire Bible, but no one in this room has memorized the entire Bible. So what's the difference between the devil's faith in God and your faith in God?"

After a brief moment of silence, a homeless man who was sitting on the floor next to his backpack said, "Authentic faith in God leads to our obedience in Christ. Because the devil has no desire to serve Christ, he's not going to be saved by his faith in Christ."

"That's a great answer," Matthew said, "and that's exactly what this verse says. If you truly know Jesus as the Lord of your life, then you are going to want to obey all of his commandments. If for some reason you are not obeying all of God's commandments, then maybe there's some kind of spiritual issue going on in your life. If that's the case, I would like to pray with you and help you work through those issues so that you can pass the self-examination test and accomplish God's will in your lives.

"Because we are running out of time, I would like to close with one of my favorite verses from the First Letter of John, which says, 'Whoever says, "I abide in him," ought to walk just as he walked.'[68]

"If you are not walking the walk just like Jesus did, you may want to spend some time this week meditating on the First Letter of John to see if there are any changes the Lord is calling you to make in your life so that you can accomplish God's will in your life."

At the end of the service, after the missionaries finished ministering to eleven homeless men who came forward for prayer, Michelle went downstairs to see if anyone in the cafeteria wanted to sell their cardboard sign. Because eight men were sitting at a round table near the stairs, Michelle approached the group, and after explaining why she was looking for the most creative and artistic signs, an older gentleman refused to take her money and gave her a cardboard sign that read, 'Can You Spare Some Change?'

When the other homeless men and women who were eating lunch in the cafeteria realized that Michelle was looking for cardboard signs, everybody started offering to give away their signs for free. She stopped by every table to receive a generous outpouring of love as she complemented her friends on their creativity. After collecting a handful of signs, she went back upstairs to show Matthew who said, "Where did you get all those?"

"They wanted to bless me," Michelle said. "It was making them feel good to be able to give me something for all that we have given to them."

"I like this one the best," Matthew said, looking through the collection. "'Why Lie, I Need a Beer.'"

"I couldn't refuse any of their gifts," Michelle said as she held up another sign that read, 'Before You Turn Away, Put Yourself in my Place.' "They were so happy to be able to give us something that we needed."

"'My ex-wife had a better lawyer,'" Matthew said as he held up another tattered piece of cardboard. "Here's another one that I like, 'Let's do Lunch—U Buy,' or how about this one, 'Please buy me a burger before I get arrested for holding this sign.'"

"A man named Randy who has been riding freight trains back and forth between San Francisco and Philadelphia for the past twelve years said he would look around this week to see if he could get me some more signs," Michelle said.

* * *

Several days later, when the missionaries arrived at the Rescue Mission for the next chapel service, three

homeless men remembered that Michelle was looking for cardboard signs and gave her more donations as they entered the building. When it came time for Matthew to deliver his message, he took hold of the microphone and said to the audience, "Please turn with me to the Book of Romans.

"In the first chapter, Saint Paul says, 'Ever since the creation of the world his eternal power and divine nature, invisible though they are, have been understood and seen through the things he has made. So they are without excuse; for though they knew God, they did not honor him as God or give thanks to him, but they became futile in their thinking, and their senseless minds were darkened. Claiming to be wise, they became fools; and they exchanged the glory of the immortal God for images resembling a mortal human being or birds or four-footed animals or reptiles.'[69]

"In this passage, Saint Paul is saying that we can look at creation and know that God exists by the things he has made. I realize there are many people in the audience today who don't believe in God's existence, so I wanted to take a look at three examples from God's creation to see if we have enough evidence to prove God's existence.

"The first example that I wanted to present to you comes from my wristwatch. Although God didn't create my watch, we know that this watch didn't create itself. If we were to take my watch apart, we would find a lot of very complex parts. There would be many gears and sprockets that need to work together in perfect harmony in order to keep the correct time.

"The same can be said about our universe. In the same way that my watch didn't create itself, we know that our universe didn't create itself, because like my watch, many complex parts are all dependent on each other. So the only logical conclusion would be that our universe came from an all-powerful creator and sustainer that we call God.

"Because there are many people in the audience who have never had an encounter with God, I wanted to ask you: Where do you think our universe came from?"

After pausing momentarily to see if anyone wanted to answer the question, Matthew continued by saying, "The most common explanation is a giant explosion in space, often called the *big bang theory*. Although no one seems to know what would cause an explosion in space, every time I light a firecracker, the explosion always causes destruction and disorder, not perfect harmony.

"When we look at our universe, we can see that it was created in perfect harmony. For example, the earth spins on its axis and orbits the sun with clock-like precision. In fact, it's better than clock-like precision, because we need an atomic clock to keep accurate time. All the clocks in my apartment are always running a little too fast or a little too slow, and I need to adjust them once a year just to keep up with the perfect, clock-like precision of the earth's orbit around the sun.

"If our planet were any closer to the sun, we would

burn up. If we were any further away from the sun, we would freeze to death. If our moon were any larger or closer to our planet, it would cause gigantic tidal waves that would destroy all the beaches and coastlines.

"Because Jupiter has one hundred times more surface area than the earth, it creates a gravitational pull that prevents almost all asteroids from hitting our planet. One explanation for all this brilliant engineering, clock-like precision and perfect harmony is a giant explosion in space, or another explanation comes from the Book of Genesis where 'God created the heavens and the earth.'[70]

"The second example comes from the periodic table. If you remember from science class, there are one hundred and eighteen basic elements in our world. These elements don't have life and free will in and of themselves. The human body is also comprised of elements from the periodic table. We are made of oxygen, hydrogen, nitrogen, carbon, calcium and sodium.

"These elements don't have life and free will in and of themselves, so there has to be something else inside of our bodies that is bringing us to life. The best option to explain this comes from the Book of Genesis when 'God formed man from the dust of the ground, and breathed into his nostrils the breath of life; and the man became a living being.'[71]

"The third example comes from evolution. There are many evolutionists who will say that humans evolved from monkeys, that monkeys evolved from reptiles, and that reptiles evolved from ameba. They say that a single-celled organism—that reproduces by splitting in half—mutated in such a way that these mutations caused even more mutations, and eventually, an ameba turned into a tadpole. After the tadpole mutated into a fish, it became a monkey, and today, human beings are nothing more than highly evolved monkeys.

"The problem with this explanation, that we didn't know about when Darwin published his theories of evolution in 1859, came almost a hundred years later with the discovery of DNA. When James Watson and Francis Crick discovered the double-helix structure of DNA in the 1950s, it took scientists another decade to realize that DNA contains all the information necessary to create a fully functioning organism. Although an ameba can reproduce by splitting itself in half, it still has DNA, which works like highly advanced computer programming code.

"In order for an ameba to mutate into a tadpole, someone would need to rewrite its genetic code. Because amebas don't have eyes or eyesight, the ameba would need to invent something that it never knew existed.

"The ameba would need to say to itself, 'I would like to create pupils, optic nerves and a brain so that my brain could read messages from my optic nerves to help me see underwater.' In order for an ameba to mutate into a tadpole that has fully functioning eyesight, someone would need to rewrite its genetic code.

"Because amebas don't have the intelligence or

ability to alter its own DNA, or the ability to rewrite or change its own genetic code, a better explanation comes from the Book of Genesis when God said, '"Let the waters bring forth swarms of living creatures, and let birds fly above the earth across the dome of the sky." So God created the great sea monsters and every living creature that moves, of every kind, with which the waters swarm, and every winged bird of every kind. And God saw that it was good.'[72]

"In all three of these examples, everybody in this room has a choice to make: We can believe that the universe created itself and that humans are nothing more than highly evolved monkeys, or we can believe what the Bible says about creation. If you want to know what the Bible says about your life, it's very simple: We have a loving God who wants to enter into a relationship with us. God created our lives with a specific purpose and plan in mind, and God wants to work in partnership with us to accomplish his purpose and plan in our lives.

"Now, both of these choices will require faith. I think it takes a lot more faith to believe in evolution because of all the inconsistencies and improbabilities, and a lot less faith to believe in God's existence. It will also be a lot easier to believe in God's existence once you have an actual encounter with God.

"When a man or a woman has never had an encounter with God, that person doesn't know what to believe, but when God makes himself very real and introduces himself to you, your spiritual eyes will be opened.

"I would like to challenge everyone in this room to ask God to make himself very real to you. There's nothing to fear. We have an all-powerful, all-knowing, loving God who wants to enter into an authentic relationship with you. God has great plans for your life, but he's not going to violate anyone's free will or force himself on anyone. God has been waiting for your invitation.

"So this week, I would like to challenge you to ask God to make himself very real to you. Once God introduces himself, you can then enter into an authentic relationship with him by accepting the Gospel message. Once you accept the Gospel message, your sins will be forgiven and you will receive the gift of the Holy Spirit."

* * *

When the demonic spirits that had been assigned to interfere with the chapel service at the Rescue Mission realized the effects this message was having on the audience, a spirit of violence rushed toward the stage in an attempt to attack Matthew while he was preaching. Before the demonic spirit could touch him, several of Matthew's guardian angels drew their swords and cut the demon into tiny pieces. When the other demonic spirits saw what happened, they departed through the roof of the building and reported the incident to Narco-Leóna.

Several of Matthew's guardian angels followed the demonic spirits into the atmosphere and said, "You are not allowed to interfere with the missionaries or we will execute judgment upon you immediately."

When the demonic spirits entered Narco-Leóna's presence, a commander said, "We just lost Nija the Destroyer. Several warriors cut him into pieces while the monkey was preaching."

"Why did you allow that to happen?" Narco-Leóna asked.

"We couldn't stop it," one of the demons said. "It happened very fast."

"We haven't been able to hinder his ministry efforts either," another demonic spirit said. "Every time we try to cause a disturbance in the audience, the big baboon takes authority over the entire room and all of our efforts fail to produce any results."

"Have you tried creating a medical emergency?" Narco-Leóna asked.

"Several times," another demonic spirit said. "On one occasion, a whiskey-pig fell off his chair and was foaming at the mouth. Everybody around him started screaming, 'Seizure!' It happened during his altar call, but the big baboon just took authority over the room and asked everybody to start praying for the man. Almost instantaneously, the drunkard regained consciousness. The entire event only lasted a few minutes, and then he went right back to preaching as if nothing had happened."

"We also started a fire in the back of the chapel while he was preaching," another demon said. "A gutter-punk was playing with his lighter, so we interfered with his thoughts and inspired him to warm up his hands by starting a pile of newspapers on fire. It created a lot of smoke and a major distraction, but it didn't last very long because another wino sitting next to him extinguished the flames with his water bottle."

"If we can't hinder their ministry efforts, and if we can't assault the missionaries directly without being slaughtered, we will need to attack them through the people they are trying to help," Narco-Leóna said.

"What do you want us to do?" one of the demonic spirits asked.

"Let's make them feel very comfortable coming down here late at night," Narco-Leóna said. "After they start feeling safe and secure, we will give them more reasons to venture deeper into the back alleyways. When the perfect opportunity arises, I will summon a spirit of violence to influence a criminal who has just been released from prison. Another option would be to summon our sexual spirits of perversion to go after the female chimpanzee."

"We will deploy both strategies," a commander said as the spirits departed.

*   *   *

After the missionaries finished answering many serious and difficult questions from a group of atheists and agnostics who surrounded them after the service, Matthew said, "Were you able to get any more signs?"

"Several creative ones," Michelle said, unfolding a large sign. "'Need help! Lost my Weed in a Series of Small Fires.' Another sign that Randy gave me reads,

'Traveling broke, but living by faith.' Here's a good one, 'My mom told me to wait here—that was fifteen years ago,' or how about this one, 'Need Cash for Alcohol Research Project.'"

"Did you set up an appointment to meet with Monica at the art gallery?" Matthew asked.

"Jclub has an event at the art gallery on the first weekend of March, so I was planning to arrive early and present our fundraising idea at that time," Michelle said.

"Very good," Matthew said. "Would you like to get together for a moonlight, mountaintop experience?"

"What did you have in mind?" Michelle asked.

"I have been working on some creative dinner ideas," Matthew said. "There's a national park on top of Meadowlark Mountain that I would like to visit. You're not allowed to have open fires, but it's okay to use a barbecue grill so long as the fire is enclosed inside of a metal container. I was thinking we could make a small campfire inside of my hibachi grill, and I will bring along some lawn chairs and blankets so we can watch the moon rise over the horizon."

"That sounds very romantic," Michelle said.

7th CHAPTER

When Matthew stopped by Mrs. Nobility's house to pick up his fiancée for the moonlight mountaintop experience, Michelle said, "I wasn't able to stop for lunch today because of my Bible study group in the morning. Then in the afternoon, I needed to attend a Jclub event at the Community College."

"I was hoping you would be hungry for dinner," Matthew said. "I have been experimenting with different types of sauces using orange juice because it's thick, sweet and tangy. In one of the recipes, I used frozen orange juice, ginger and sesame seeds, and in another one, I used teriyaki and minced garlic.

"After we start a fire and let it burn down into a hot bed of coals, I wanted to load up some metal shish kebab skewers with precooked chicken tenders and an assortment of vegetables. Because the chicken is already cooked, all we need to do is warm it up, along with the vegetables, and then we can dip our shish kebabs into six different sauces to see which one you like best."

"That sounds delightful," Michelle said.

After driving forty-five minutes, the missionaries reached the top of Meadowlark Mountain and found the perfect campsite location overlooking the city lights below.

Halfway through dinner, Matthew said, "I have some more information to share with you about why Catholics visit the Sacrament of Reconciliation. Before we get into why Catholics confess their sins to a man inside a tiny dark room, I would like to define two types of sins: mortal and venial.

"This classification comes from the First Letter of John where the Apostle said, 'There is sin that is mortal.'[73] He also says 'All wrongdoing is sin, but there is sin that is not mortal.'[74] From this Scripture passage we know that some sins are mortal, meaning they lead to death, and there are some sins that do not lead to death, which we call venial.

"Saint Paul gives us a list of mortal sins in his letter to the Galatians when he said, 'I am warning you, as I warned you before: those who do such things will not inherit the kingdom of God.'[75] The list of mortal sins listed in Galatians includes fornication, idolatry, witch-craft and drunkenness.

"Saint Paul also says in his First Letter to the Corinthians, 'Do you not know that wrongdoers will not inherit the kingdom of God? Do not be deceived! Fornicators, idolaters, adulterers, male prostitutes, sodomites, thieves, the greedy, drunkards, revilers, rob-bers—none of these will inherit the kingdom of God.'[76]

"Other smaller sins would include being rude to someone at the department store or coveting another person's employment status or income. All sin is an agreement with evil, but when Catholics commit a smaller venial sin, they don't need to go to confession. We are free to confess our venial sins directly to God.

"The problem with mortal sins is that they lead to the death of a person's relationship with God. Once a person commits a mortal sin, it's very difficult to break free from that cycle. This is especially true for sexual sins.

When a young couple commits the sin of fornication, demonic sexual spirits gain access to that couple's lives and hinder that couple's relationship with God.

"Once a couple commits the sin of fornication, they can confess their sins directly to God by saying, 'I'm so very sorry,' but deep in their hearts, they are probably not truly sorry. That's because most people enjoy their sins, and soon a destructive pattern is formed. These people will have sex outside of a God-approved marriage and afterward say, 'I'm sorry,' then they will have more sex and say, 'I'm sorry again,' and soon they find themselves in a very destructive cycle of constant sin and never-ending repentance.

"To solve this problem and break free from this destructive cycle, the young couple that has been ensnared in sexual bondage needs help from another person who is not ensnared in the same sinful pattern. That is why the Book of James says, 'Confess your sins to one another, and pray for one another, so that you may be healed.'[77] If the young couple attended a Catholic church, they would go to confession; but if they attended a mainstream Protestant church, where would they go to get help?"

"One option would be to seek assistance from an accountability partner or a prayer partner," Michelle said. "Another option would be to seek help from a Christian counselor or an elder from the church."

"The young couple could also confess their sins to a Bible study group," Matthew said, "but think about how difficult that would be. Imagine the courage it would take for a young woman to show up at your weekly Bible study meeting and say, 'I'm so very sorry, my dear sisters in Christ. I feel like such a pathetic hypocrite. I have been having sex with my boyfriend on a regular basis, and even though I sin and confess, I'm stuck in a destructive cycle and can't seem to break free.'

"If the young woman went to your Bible study group and said that, I'm sure all the women would gather around her and pray for deliverance. They would drive the devil out of her life as they interceded on her behalf. A minor form of exorcism would occur that day, and the young woman would receive grace, along with the spiritual power and strength that she needed to break free from that destructive cycle of sin.

"That's exactly what occurs inside the confessional, except it's easier, convenient and private. Just imagine all the damage that would occur if the young woman maintained a leadership role in her church, or if she was a leader in the Bible study group.

"I'm sure the other women in the group would pray for her deliverance, but some of the women may also lose respect for her. If she ever tried to give another woman spiritual advice, the other women in the group may treat her like Mary Magdalene and say, 'Who are you to give us spiritual advice? Just last month you were fornicating with your boyfriend, and now you want to be all spiritual.'

"Confessing your sins to a priest in the confessional

is easier than trying to find a Christian counselor, church elder or spiritual mentor. Every Catholic Church in America has confession times posted on their website, and it's easy to find a convenient time and location so that you can travel to a nearby parish, where nobody knows who you are, to take advantage of a powerful and effective Sacrament."

"All that sounds well and good," Michelle said, "but what about the part where the priest forgives your sins and grants you absolution?"

"In the Gospel of Mark, there's a passage about a paralyzed man who was being carried along by a group of his friends," Matthew said. "When these men reached the house where Jesus was speaking, they wanted to enter, but there wasn't any room, so they removed a section of the roof and lowered the paralyzed man down by ropes in front of Jesus.

"When Jesus saw their faith, he said to the paralytic, 'Son, your sins are forgiven.'[78]

"When the scribes and Pharisees heard this, they said to themselves, 'It is blasphemy! Who can forgive sins but God alone?'[79]

"When Jesus perceived in his spirit what they were discussing among themselves, he said to them, '"Which is easier, to say to the paralytic, 'Your sins are forgiven,' or to say, 'Stand up and take your mat and walk'? But so that you may know that the Son of Man has authority on earth to forgive sins"—he said to the paralytic—"I say to you, stand up, take your mat and go to your home."'[80]

Immediately, the paralyzed man was healed and he was able to rise up off the mat. When the crowds saw this miracle, 'they were filled with awe, and they glorified God, who had given such authority to human beings.'[81]

"From this passage, we can see that the power to forgive men's sins was passed down from God the Father to our Lord, Jesus Christ, but where did the power and ability go from there?" Matthew asked.

"I'm not sure," Michelle said.

"In the Gospel of John, when the disciples were gathered together in the upper room, Jesus appeared to them after his death and resurrection and said, '"Peace be with you. As the Father has sent me, so I send you." When he had said this, he breathed on them and said to them, "Receive the Holy Spirit. If you forgive the sins of any, they are forgiven them; if you retain the sins of any, they are retained."'[82]

"From this Scripture passage, we can see the power and ability to forgive men's sin was passed from our Lord, Jesus Christ, to the Apostles. Saint Paul also confirmed this gift in his Second Letter to the Corinthians when he said, 'All this is from God, who reconciled us to himself through Christ, and has given us the ministry of reconciliation.'[83] He then goes on to say that 'God was reconciling the world to himself, not counting their trespasses against them, and entrusting the message of reconciliation to us. So we are ambassadors for Christ, since God is making his appeal through us.'[84]

"The word *ambassador* means a high-ranking official

who represents his or her government in another country. Because Saint Paul is an ambassador for Christ, he represents Christ while participating in the ministry of reconciliation. In the same way that Saint Paul represents Christ, we are also called to represent Christ.

"A good example of this comes from the *Catechism* in a section entitled Priestly, Prophetic and Royal People of God.[85] In this section it says, 'The whole People of God participates in these three offices of Christ,' and that we bear the 'responsibilities for mission and service that flow from them.'[86] That means that all Christians represent the King, and we fulfill the office of royalty by advancing God's kingdom here on earth. We are also called to fulfill our prophetic role in Christ by speaking God's truth to all people. We fulfill our priestly role in Christ by reconciling sinners back to God.

"So let's look at how these three offices of priest, prophet and king would work in your women's Bible study group. Let's say a young woman comes to your group and pretends that everything is perfectly fine in her life. You know something is wrong because the Holy Spirit has given you a powerful gift of discernment, so you keep asking her questions.

"Finally, she breaks down and starts crying. She confesses the sin of fornication with her boyfriend. It has been going on for over a year and she feels terrible. She can act happy and pretend to be holy on the outside, but deep inside her heart, she is dying a slow and painful death. How would you minister to this woman?"

"We would love her, listen to her, pray with her and encourage her," Michelle said.

"If the young woman confessed her sins and said a sinner's prayer by accepting Jesus' sacrifice on the cross for the forgiveness of her sins, would you be able to reassure this woman of Jesus' love and forgiveness?"

"Of course I would," Michelle said.

"That's exactly what happens inside of the confessional," Matthew said, "except it's a lot more powerful and effective because the Sacrament of Reconciliation imparts spiritual power that helps the penitent avoid the temptations of sin in the future.

"When I go to confession, I can feel the difference. Some priests can impart better blessings than others. I'm not sure if this has something to do with the priest's own personal level of holiness or the amount of faith the priest has as an ambassador of Christ."

"What's it like going to confession?" Michelle asked.

"I like the Sacrament because it's powerful and effective," Matthew said, "although nobody really enjoys going to confession because it's humbling and humiliating to confess your sins to another person. In older churches, there's a small, dark room with a dim light on the wall so you can see what you're doing. In modern churches, there's a larger room with two chairs so you can sit down and personally visit with a priest.

"Catholics call this face-to-face confession. There's also a partition between the priest's chair and the door, so you can give your confession behind a screened partition if you want to hide your identity and protect your privacy.

"I usually start by telling the priest how long it has been since my last confession, and then give him a list of my sins. Sometimes the priest will ask questions about my sins or give me spiritual advice on how to avoid my sins in the future."

"Can you give me an example?" Michelle asked.

"Last month I went to confession and told the priest I was struggling with negative and angry thoughts," Matthew said. "He asked me about their source, and because I didn't know the answer, I told him it was probably coming from the news media and all the negative events that are constantly going on all around us. After he gave me some spiritual advice on how to renew my thoughts in Christ, he asked me to say an Act of Contrition."

"What's that?" Michelle asked.

"It's a prayer where sinners say, 'Oh my God, I am heartily sorry for having offended you. I detest all my sins because of your just punishment, but most of all because they offend you, my Lord God who is worthy of all my love. I firmly resolve with the help of your grace to sin no more and avoid the near occasions of sin.'

"There are many different versions of this prayer, but the penitent is always praying directly to God and never to the priest. After I confess my sins and make an act of contrition, the priest will give me a form of penance to perform. When I told the priest I was struggling with negative thoughts, he wanted me to avoid watching the news media all week and to spend that time reading my Bible.

"After I agreed to perform the act of penance, the priest granted me absolution by saying, 'God, the Father of mercies, through the death and resurrection of his Son has reconciled the world to himself and sent the Holy Spirit among us for the forgiveness of sins; through the ministry of the Church may God grant you pardon and peace, and I absolve you from your sins in the name of the Father, Son and Holy Spirit.'

"During the absolution, when the priest makes the sign of the cross, I can feel the power of the Holy Spirit washing over me and giving me the spiritual strength that I need to be more holy. I don't like going to confession because it's so humbling, but I love how I feel afterward. I love the power, grace and freedom that I receive from this Sacrament, and I think you should give it a try."

"I would like that," Michelle said. "Can non-Catholics participate in the Sacrament of Reconciliation?"

"I'm not sure," Matthew said. "That's why Clergyman O'Connor wants to sign you up for RCIA classes."

"The more I learn about the Catholic faith, the more questions I have," Michelle said.

"I think I have addressed all of your concerns, except for purgatory and the rapture," Matthew said.

"Do we have time tonight?" Michelle asked as she

put more sticks on the fire. "It looks like the moon is about to rise over the horizon, and I don't have any appointments tomorrow, so I'm okay with staying out late tonight."

8th CHAPTER

Missionaries

"Before we discuss purgatory, I wanted to share with you a testimony from a guy I met who was living underneath a bridge near the highway," Matthew said. "His name is Donald, and a few days after I preached a message for the atheists and agnostics, Donald had a powerful encounter with the Lord.

"He had been out drinking late that night and was so intoxicated that the staff at the Mission didn't want to let him in the building. After Donald begged and pleaded with them for a very long time, they finally let him inside and gave him a mat on the floor. Before Donald passed out that evening, he prayed a simple prayer by saying, 'If there is a God out there, I need help.'

"When Donald woke up the following morning, he felt different. During the night he had vomited and urinated on himself, so he would have normally been in a very bad mood, but that morning he knew something had changed, because he could feel a newfound sense of peace and inner strength deep within his heart.

"You should have seen him standing on the sidewalk, he was radiating with joy. From that point forward, Donald stopped drinking and has been clean and sober ever since. When I asked him if he was attending a local church, he told me he started going to Alcoholics Anonymous meetings."

"Praise God," Michelle said. "We should pray for Donald to find a good sponsor so that he can work through the twelve steps."

"You know a lot more about Alcoholics Anonymous than I do," Matthew said. "I have only attended a few meetings to see what was going on, but during the sessions that I have attended, there was a group of men and women sitting in a circle. After the meeting began, a man introduced himself as an alcoholic and started a profanity-laced rant about all the things in life that he was unhappy about.

"Other people in the group were drinking coffee and chain-smoking cigarettes. When that man finished venting all his negativity, another person continued the conversation in the same direction. I'm not sure how attending ninety meetings in ninety days is going to help Donald, but I was hoping you could explain that to me."

"The founding members of Alcoholics Anonymous were Christians who took spiritual principles from the Bible to help people get clean and sober," Michelle said.

"Why do they introduce themselves as alcoholics?" Matthew asked.

"Most alcoholics spend the majority of their lives

trying to convince themselves and others that they do not have a drinking problem," Michelle said. "So to hear an alcoholic admit that he or she has a drinking problem is a good thing. It would be similar to a Christian admitting that they are sinners and in need of a Savior on a regular basis."

"My concern with Donald attending Alcoholics Anonymous meetings instead of a Bible-based church is that his prayer didn't sound very Christian," Matthew said. "'If there is a God out there, I need help.' I'm assuming that after Donald said a prayer asking God to make himself very real, God showed up, and after introducing himself, God gave Donald the internal strength that he needed to stop drinking. I'm not sure how long Donald's sobriety will last, because the devil can come along at any moment and poke his emotional wounds and drive him back to the bottle."

"That's why Donald needs to start working the twelve steps," Michelle said. "One of their favorite sayings is, 'It works if you work it.' I would like to see Donald attending a Bible-based church as well, but very few people in our modern-day, mainstream churches will understand what Donald is going through.

"If Donald finds a good sponsor and starts working the steps, he will need to take a spiritual inventory of his life. Once he evaluates his past, he will need to forgive all the people from his past who have hurt him, and he will also need to make amends for all of his actions that have harmed other people."

"Now that we have established how the twelve-step program would be helpful for Donald to maintain his sobriety, let's take a look at how his situation would apply to purgatory," Matthew said. "First of all, purgatory is a part of heaven. When a person dies, there are only two eternal destinations—heaven or hell. If Donald were to pass away tonight, I'm assuming he would go to heaven because he had an authentic encounter with God on the chapel floor, but he still has a lot of internal healing work to do."

"A lot of drug addicts and alcoholics have been deeply wounded," Michelle said.

"You make a good point that the homeless have been deeply wounded and need a lot of emotional healing work before they can fully enjoy living with God in heaven for all eternity," Matthew said. "Our need for sanctification comes from many examples in the Bible, starting with the Book of Leviticus where God says, 'You shall be holy, for I am holy.'[87] Jesus says the same thing in the Gospel of Matthew, 'Be perfect, therefore, as your heavenly Father is perfect.'[88] The Apostle Peter makes the same point by saying, 'As he who called you is holy, be holy yourselves in all your conduct.'[89]

"In the Book of Revelation, the Apostle John says that nothing unclean shall enter heaven.[90] The Book of Hebrews says, 'Pursue peace with everyone, and the holiness without which no one will see the Lord.'[91]

"Other Bible passages speak about how it's not possible for a person to be saved except through fire.

For example, in the First Letter to the Corinthians, Saint Paul is talking about pastors who were proclaiming a false message. When their work is tested, they may be saved, but only through fire.[92] Other Bible passages that point toward the existence of purgatory comes from our need to forgive other people. In the Gospel of Matthew, Jesus ties our own forgiveness to the way we forgive other people by saying, 'If you do not forgive others, neither will your Father forgive your trespasses.'[93]

"When Peter asks Jesus, 'If another member of the church sins against me, how often should I forgive?'[94] Jesus answered the question with a parable about a king who settled accounts with his slaves. At the end of the parable, the king who represents Jesus says, '"I forgave you all that debt because you pleaded with me. Should you not have had mercy on your fellow slave, as I had mercy on you?" And in anger his lord handed him over to be tortured until he would pay his entire debt. So my heavenly Father will also do to every one of you, if you do not forgive your brother or sister from your heart.'[95]

"In another Bible passage, Jesus says, 'Why do you not judge for yourselves what is right? Thus, when you go with your accuser before a magistrate, on the way make an effort to settle the case, or you may be dragged before the judge, and the judge hand you over to the officer, and the officer throw you in prison. I tell you, you will never get out until you have paid the very last penny.'[96]

"So from all these Scripture passages, we can see

that God is perfectly holy and that nothing unholy can enter into his presence. We can also see that some people will be required to pay a penalty for their sins through a refining fire, and they will not be able to get out of prison until they pay the last penny.

"In Donald's situation, we know that he has some inner healing work to accomplish. Maybe some people from his past have hurt him and he still needs to work through the forgiveness process. If Donald's life on earth ended tonight, there would be several options for purification before he could fully enjoy heaven. One option would be that Donald could take all of his emotional baggage, sinful desires and lack of forgiveness with him into heaven. If this were the case, when God looked at Donald, he wouldn't see the true condition of his heart, but only the blood of Christ that was shed on the cross of Calvary."

"That option reminds me of the time when Jesus rebuked the Pharisees for being whitewashed tombs," Michelle said as she removed her phone from her pocket. "I think it's in the Gospel of Matthew. 'Woe to you, scribes and Pharisees, hypocrites! For you are like whitewashed tombs, which on the outside look beautiful, but inside they are full of the bones of the dead and of all kinds of filth. So you also on the outside look righteous to others, but inside you are full of hypocrisy and lawlessness.'"[97]

"Why would Jesus condemn the Pharisees for being whitewashed tombs that look beautiful on the outside, but in reality are full of filth and lawlessness, and at the same time allow people like Donald into heaven when they are driven by self-destruction, consumed with emotional wounds, and suffer from the lack of forgiveness?" Matthew asked.

"That doesn't make sense to me," Michelle said. "I can't imagine heaven being filled with all the people from recovery groups who are constantly craving a cigarette, looking around for something to get high on and speaking with a constant stream of profanities flowing out of their mouths."

"I had a preacher present that concept to me during a Bible study group," Matthew said. "For his speaking props, he had a picture of a sinful man, and when he placed a red transparent piece of film over the man, a red cross appeared. He used this analogy to say that's how God is going to see us when we die and go to heaven. God will no longer look at all our sinful desires buried deep within our hearts; he will only see the blood of Christ covering us, similar to the Pharisees whom Jesus condemned for being hypocrites and whitewashed tombs."

"What's the other option for Donald's situation when he goes to heaven?" Michelle asked.

"Another option would be that Jesus could violate Donald's free will and make him forgive all the people from his past who have hurt him," Matthew said. "Maybe the second that Donald dies and enters heaven his entire past would be washed clean, and he would instantly become holy as God is holy. This option doesn't make sense to me, because when a man or woman has an encounter with Jesus and is filled with the Holy Spirit, it doesn't mean that God violates that person's free will and makes them forgive all the people from their past who have hurt them.

"Even the most holy of all Christians still struggle with temptations and need to forgive people from their past. So if God doesn't make a person perfectly holy when they become a Christian, why would he make them perfectly holy after they die?"

"What's the other option for Donald's situation?" Michelle asked.

"The most logical explanation would be a purification stage of heaven where Donald could work through all of his unresolved issues so that he could enter into God's presence," Matthew said. "Because nothing unholy can enter into God's presence, Donald will either need to work through the process of sanctification while he's still here on earth, or else he will need to work through that process before he can enter into heaven."

"Although the concept of purgatory is not clearly defined in Scripture, I like the idea of a purification stage of heaven for several reasons," Michelle said. "First of all, it would motivate believers to work out their salvation with fear and trembling while they still have time left here on earth. It would also serve as a spiritual washroom where the Lord's servants could get cleaned up in before meeting the great King.

"When I think about Donald's situation, I picture a man who has been fighting the devil for many years in a very dark and hostile environment. If I were in Donald's situation—and just came out of a major battle with the devil and was covered with all the filth that we see on skid row—I would want a washroom to get cleaned up in before entering into God's presence."

"There's a parable in the Gospel of Matthew that describes our need for sanctification before meeting the great King," Matthew said. "It's located in the twenty-second chapter where the great King held a banquet for his Son. When the King sent his servants to invite all the important dignitaries, they started making excuses, so the King turned to the common people and invited everyone. After the King's servants went out into the highway and byways, they gathered everybody they could find so that the wedding hall would be filled with guests.[98]

"When the King came to meet the guests, he noticed a man who was not wearing a wedding robe and said to him, 'Friend, how did you get in here without a wedding robe?'[99] Because the man was speechless, the King said to his servants, 'Bind him hand and foot, and throw him into the outer darkness, where there will be weeping and gnashing of teeth.'[100]

"Some theologians think this passage represents the wedding feast of the Lamb as described in the Book of Revelation, while other theologians say it represents a spiritual reality here on earth. In either event, it's important to be holy as God is holy, to work out our salvation with fear and trembling and to accomplish God's will in our lives, which is our sanctification."[101]

"I wish we could stay here all night," Michelle said. "It's so peaceful, I could fall asleep in this lawn chair, wrapped up in these warm blankets underneath the star-filled night sky."

"Maybe we could bring our camping tents up here when it gets warmer," Matthew said as he emptied the contents of his water bottle on the hot coals. "I would like to pack everything that we need for our mission trip inside our backpacks to see if it will fit. If our backpacks are not too heavy, we could park a couple of miles down the road and hike up here to spend the night."

"That sounds like a learning experience," Michelle said. "Another option would be to park your 4Runner at the campsite and then hike a mile or two up the canyon. That way we would have a vehicle close to us during the night."

"Better to learn our lessons the easy way while we are still in the planning and preparation stage than to learn them the hard way halfway around the world," Matthew said.

* * *

Later that evening, when Matthew was driving back down the mountain, Michelle asked, "Would you like to go shopping with me and some homeless women at the thrift store after the chapel service on Monday?"

"I was planning to preach on work ethic," Matthew

said. "Then after the service, I want to hire a few guys to pick up trash for several hours."

"I promised to take Amber shopping on Monday," Michelle said. "Maybe while you are picking up trash, we could go shopping."

"You know I don't like letting you out of my sight when we're working down there," Matthew said. "Even though our reputation has grown, and everybody knows who we are, it's still a very dangerous neighborhood."

"Can you reschedule the trash pick-up project for another day and go shopping with us on Monday?" Michelle asked.

"Then I wouldn't have anything to preach about on Monday," Matthew said. "How about we compromise and create a list of rules that govern our relationship?"

"What kind of rules?" Michelle asked.

"Do you remember when you made me promise to never invite a homeless person into my apartment to live with me?" Matthew asked.

"I remember," Michelle said.

"I would like to expand that rule so that we never invite homeless people, drug addicts or alcoholics into our homes to live with us; and because we both have the right to add to these rules at any time, I would like to add lemurs and any other wild animals to the list," Matthew said.

"That's not fair," Michelle said. "Lemurs are so soft, friendly and adorable."

"Our next rule would be that we both agree to

never get separated when we are working with the homeless, ministering in a dangerous neighborhood, or traveling for an international mission trip."

"I agree to those rules," Michelle said. "Can I add my own rules to govern the terms of our relationship?"

"We are both free to add to our list of rules at any time, so long as they are mutually agreed upon," Matthew said. "If there's an issue going on in my life or something that I'm doing that's reckless or dangerous or has the potential to harm myself or others, then all you need to do is bring it to my attention so that we can add it to our list."

"I'll work on rule number three tomorrow," Michelle said as she gave her fiancé a kiss good night.

9th CHAPTER

When the missionaries arrived at the Rescue Mission for the Monday afternoon chapel service, Michelle began greeting the guests at the entrance and collecting more signs, while Matthew played a CD and prayer-walked the perimeter of the chapel. When it was time for the message to begin, Matthew turned off the praise and worship music and began his sermon by saying, "Please turn with me to the Book of Proverbs.

"In the sixth chapter, God's Word says, 'Go to the ant, you lazybones; consider its ways, and be wise. Without having any chief or officer or ruler, it prepares its food in summer, and gathers its sustenance in harvest. How long will you lie there, O lazybones? When will you rise from your sleep? A little sleep, a little slumber, a little folding of the hands to rest, and poverty will come upon you like a robber, and want, like an armed warrior.'[102]

"There are only six verses in this passage and I would like to unpack them very carefully because they contain a wealth of wisdom. Before we discuss the work ethic of ants, I wanted to ask everyone in this room what it's like to have *want* come on you like an armed warrior. We all know what an encounter with an armed warrior would be like, but what's it like to have poverty come on you like an armed warrior?"

Because no one in the chapel wanted to answer the question, Matthew said, "If you don't want poverty to come upon you like an armed warrior, then all you need to do is study the work ethic of ants.

"When I was a little boy, I would intentionally mess up anthills, and a few seconds later, there would be a swarm of ants coming out of the ground to defend the colony and start the rebuilding process. It didn't matter how big the anthill was because I could totally mess up a very large mound, and the next day, it would be completely rebuilt.

"Ants are very impressive workers because they can carry ten times their body weight. Leafcutter ants can carry up to thirty times their body weight while hanging upside down on a tree branch. That would be similar to a two-hundred-pound man carrying a cow on his back while climbing up a redwood tree. They can also travel two inches per second, which is the equivalent of ten feet per minute, in an attempt to find food.

"They also have the ability to lay down a chemical scent trail so they can find their way back to the colony. They work hard all day long for the well-being of the colony, they never complain, they never get drunk and never need any kind of instructions, supervision or monetary incentives. They work very hard helping to provide for the needs of others, all because God programmed them that way.

"So if you want to be a successful businessman or businesswoman, all you need to do is study the work ethic of ants, because they are smart enough to gather all the food they need during the summer months, so they can stay warm and well fed deep underground during the winter months.

"The opposite work ethic of an ant is described in verse nine that says, 'How long will you lie there, O lazybones? When will you rise from your sleep?'[103] Although the Bible contains many warnings about being lazy, I continue to hear people say, 'Take it easy, man,' and 'Don't work too hard.' If we were all given a dollar every time someone said, 'Take it easy' or 'Don't work too hard,' we would all be millionaires.

"The question I wanted to ask you today is: What's wrong with work?"

After a long moment of silence, a man standing in the back of the room said, "Because you are helping other people get rich."

"Why can't you work for yourselves?" Matthew asked.

"Because it takes money to make money," another man said.

"I have a challenge that I would like to present you with today," Matthew said. "It's very simple. All you need is a piece of paper and a pencil, because I would like everybody to make a list of things to do.

"I have a list of things to do, and I'm constantly looking at my list to see what I can accomplish. I like working hard because it makes me feel successful and productive. I have a very difficult time sitting around all day long doing nothing. I would rather be out working and promoting God's kingdom, because God promises to provide for our needs.

"When you make a list of things to do, every item on your list can be for your own benefit. For example, I know there are many people in the audience who need to get an identification card. There are some people here today who can't get an identification card because they need a copy of their birth certificate.

"If you need a copy of your birth certificate, that's the first item I would put on your list of things to do. Item number one, get a copy of your birth certificate. Item number two, get a government identification card. Item number three, go shopping at the thrift store for some business attire. Item number four, get a good job. Item number five, open a bank account and save some money. Item number six, start your own business.

"As you can see, every item on your list of things to do will benefit yourself, but it's still okay if you need to work for the benefit of others, because people are directly compensated for their service to society. If you provide no service or benefit to society, then you will not receive any compensation. If you provide highly valued goods and services to society, then you will become very rich.

"So this week, I would like to challenge everybody to start working on a list of things to do. All you need to do is ask God for assistance, and start writing down the things you could be doing to improve your lives. When you have some free time, pick an item on your list and start working hard for yourself. Once you accomplish an item on your list, cross it off and allow yourself the ability to feel good for being self-employed and productive. Once you accomplish the first item, start working on the second item.

"On my list, I'm constantly adding new items and constantly working hard to accomplish existing items. When you start working together with God to add items to your list, you will also have the opportunity to start working in partnership with God to accomplish those items. So you see, everybody in this room has the opportunity to enter into a successful working relationship with God."

After Matthew led the audience in prayer to enter into a deeper and more prosperous relationship with the Lord, he said, "We are also looking for a few volunteers who would be willing to pick up trash for several hours this afternoon. The job doesn't pay much, but it would be a good opportunity for you to be a productive member of society."

After making the announcement, two men raised their hands, so Matthew said, "Please come forward.

Everybody else is dismissed for lunch."

As the men approached the stage, one of them said, "My name is Dillon" as he shook Matthew's hand. "Your message was a great blessing to me, so I wanted to give back to the community for all that I have been receiving."

"What's your name?" Matthew asked as he extended his hand to the other man.

"Justin," the man said.

"This is Amber and Melanie," Michelle said as she approached the stage with her friends.

"It's good to meet you," Matthew said. "If you will please follow me outside, we can get started."

When Matthew approached his 4Runner, he opened the back hatch to remove the trash bags, water bottles and rubber gloves. He said to the volunteers, "When I was speaking to the audience, I said the job didn't pay much, because if I told a large gathering of homeless men they could earn ten dollars for a few hours of work, everybody would want the job."

"There would have been a stampede," Justin said.

"Because I didn't want to create any problems, I decided to keep the compensation private so that we could work out the details ourselves," Matthew said. "So let's start with Amber and Melanie, because I know Michelle promised to take you shopping today.

"One option is that you can go shopping and Michelle will buy you ten dollars worth of clothes. A better option would be to help us pick up trash today so that you could earn ten dollars in cash, and then next Monday, we could all go clothes shopping together, and I will buy you an additional ten dollars worth of clothes."

"I would rather have the cash today," Melanie said.

"I need new clothes," Amber said, "but I'm okay to go shopping another time."

"I know you guys skipped a meal," Matthew said. "Everybody else is downstairs eating lunch and you came forward to volunteer your time, so another option is that we could spend some of your proceeds by going to your favorite restaurant afterward."

"I'm not that hungry," Justin said. "Besides the Salvation Army serves a spaghetti dinner every Monday evening, and the Rescue Mission has another hot meal at seven o'clock tonight."

"The other requirement is that everyone needs to agree that you will not use the money to buy drugs or alcohol," Matthew said. "So if everybody agrees, I thought the girls could pick up trash on one side of the street while we work on the other side."

"Make sure you keep up with us," Michelle said as the women crossed the street. "I don't want to see you guys falling behind."

After the missionaries cleaned up all the trash that was scattered on the sidewalk in front of the Rescue Mission, they headed down Madison Avenue toward the park where the majority of the homeless population resided during the day. There was so much trash in the bushes that everybody was able to fill the first bag within a very short period of time.

"This is kind of fun," Michelle said. "Once you pick up one piece, there's another, and soon you're on an endless journey."

"Where do we put the trash once our bags are full?" Melanie asked.

"There are some dumpsters in the alleyway," Dillon said. "If you want, I will stash our trash over there."

"We'll go with you," Michelle said. "It's important that we stay together."

After the group put their trash bags in the dumpster, everybody headed back to the park to clean up the remaining items before returning to the Rescue Mission. When they reached Matthew's vehicle, he took out his wallet and paid the volunteers ten dollars each.

"I would like to pray with you before you leave," Michelle said, placing her hand on Melanie's shoulder.

"It's okay, Amber," Matthew said. "You can come a little closer."

Once everybody formed a circle, Michelle said, "Oh, most gracious Heavenly Father, we thank you for our new friends, and I ask you to bless the work of their hands, fill their hearts with peace and joy, and open up the floodgates of heaven to bestow upon us every abundant blessing. In Jesus' name we pray."

"God bless you," Dillon said, turning to leave.

"I can't thank you enough," Justin said. "Here's a phone number where you can leave a message. I'm available anytime, just give me a call."

"Do you girls have phone numbers?" Michelle asked as the women stood there motionless. "I was hoping we could keep in touch. Where are you staying?"

"You know, here and there," Melanie said. "I usually stay at the Salvation Army Center when I can get a private room. Other times, I stay in the women's dorm room at the Central Presbyterian Shelter."

"Can I leave a message for you at those locations?" Michelle asked as she wrote down her cell number on the back of a Jclub business card.

"I will be on the lookout for your phone call," Melanie said as she gave Michelle a hug.

"What about you, Amber?" Michelle asked. "Where do you stay?"

"My home is over there," Amber said, pointing toward a large billboard sign.

"Will you please show us where you are staying?" Michelle asked.

After walking across the street, Amber pointed toward a piece of cardboard lying on the ground next to a chain-link fence. When the missionaries approached the location, the guard dogs on the other side of the fence started barking.

"They won't hurt you," Amber said. "They keep me company and warm at night."

"Have you thought about getting a place of your own?" Michelle asked. "I picture you in your very own studio apartment. I can see sunshine streaming through the windows. Your house is filled with God's love."

"I can't afford to pay rent," Amber said.

"All you need is a good job," Michelle said. "Maybe a little motivation and some inner healing from the Lord. I'm sure God is ready to deliver you from the streets whenever you're ready to stop drinking."

"That's never going to happen," Amber said as she walked away.

"Don't forget about our appointment on Monday," Michelle said. "You still have a ten-dollar credit to spend at the thrift store."

"What did she mean by the dogs keep her warm at night?" Matthew asked.

"I think she sleeps on that piece of cardboard and the guard dogs on the other side of the fence curl up next to her at night to keep her warm," Michelle said.

"I'm starting to feel bad," Matthew said. "She probably needed to buy some warm clothes at the thrift store."

"There wasn't enough time today," Michelle said. "I promised Daniel and Rebecca that I would help them set up the Candlelight Jazz Club tonight, and I'm already running late."

"How are we going to help Amber?" Matthew asked.

"She started opening up to me when we were picking up trash," Michelle said. "She's from a Native American tribe in Wyoming and has been an alcoholic for a very long time. She also told me she's Catholic."

"Maybe I could take her to confession," Matthew said. "It would be similar to how Alcoholics Anonymous members take an inventory of their lives so that they can make amends. In Amber's situation, she would be making a long list of all her sins so that she could confess them to God through the Sacrament of Reconciliation."

"It would also be helpful if we could get her to attend ninety meetings in ninety days," Michelle said. "If we could get her clean and sober, I'm sure we could find a government assistance program to help her pay the rent on her very own apartment."

"I like the idea of connecting people to God through repentance, helping them get clean and sober through a support group and moving them off the streets and into their own apartments," Matthew said. "How do we start this process with Amber?"

"We need to spend more time with her to develop a deeper friendship so that we can establish trust," Michelle said. "Let's pray about how to help Amber this evening, and I will stop by your apartment after the Jclub event."

"Very good," Matthew said as he kissed his fiancée goodbye.

* * *

After the demonic spirits that had been following the missionaries discovered how they wanted to help Amber, they started arguing amongst themselves about the best way to stage a late-night attack. One of the sexually perverted spirits said, "Let's assault the feather-neck late at night and get her to blame the big baboon so we can destroy his reputation."

"That will never work," a spirit of violence said. "Let's use the drunken feather-neck as bait to cause a series of late-night problems, so that when the monkeys come to her rescue, we can motivate a convict to eliminate them at gunpoint and steal their vehicle."

"I also want to get the female chimpanzee alone so that we can molest her," the commander said.

*　*　*

Later that evening, when Michelle stopped by Matthew's apartment, she said, "Because Valentine's Day is several weeks away, I was wondering if we could conduct a special service on God's extravagant love."

"What did you have in mind?" Matthew asked.

"I was talking with my friend Becky from Centerfield Elementary School this evening; and because she's an art teacher, I asked her if her kids could make Valentine's Day cards for the homeless," Michelle said. "Can you imagine all the joy that would create? We were thinking about making two hundred cards out of red, white and pink construction paper, and having her kids write personalized messages of love on them.

"Then we could take pictures of the homeless guys receiving their cards and share those photos with Becky's students. After we finish with the photography, you could preach a message on God's extravagant love and conclude your message with a call for salvation."

"That's an excellent idea," Matthew said. "I also

wanted to stop by the Regency Hotel later that evening to visit with Daniel and Rebecca for Jclub's annual Valentine's Day dance."

"I still can't believe Daniel rented the grand ballroom," Michelle said. "We already have over three hundred members registered, so it's going to be a great event."

"Did you have a chance to pray about how to help Amber?" Matthew asked.

"All we can do is keep reaching out to her," Michelle said. "We can show her God's love by taking her shopping at the thrift store. We could also take her out to lunch, and if she's willing, you could take her to confession. Let's ask her if she would be willing to attend some Alcoholics Anonymous meetings with us. If she shows signs of progress, we could also rent a cheap hotel room on the other side of town for a week to show her how nice it would be to have her own apartment."

"Why on the other side of town?" Matthew asked.

"If we get her a place near the Rescue Mission, she may invite all her drinking buddies back to the hotel room to party with her all night," Michelle said. "They may trash the hotel room and steal the television, and we could be held accountable."

"I have already learned that lesson the hard way with the fence project," Matthew said.

"I would want to see Amber making a lot of progress toward sobriety before we rent her a hotel room," Michelle said. "She would also need to display a desire for sobriety, the discipline to attend meetings, and a commitment to never drink again. If she really wanted to stop drinking, I would be happy to pay for the hotel room and help her find government assistance to pay for her own place."

"That sounds like a wise approach," Matthew said. "I will follow your lead when it comes to dealing with Amber."

"I have also learned some lessons the hard way," Michelle said. "I have spent a lot of time attending Al-Anon meetings, listening to all the horror stories."

"Would you like to get together for Chinese food Saturday night?" Matthew asked. "I was hoping we could continue our conversation on why the Catholic Church doesn't believe in the modern-day theory of the rapture."

"Instead of Chinese food, would you like to check out a new Vietnamese restaurant?" Michelle asked.

"That sounds great," Matthew said. "If you want to make reservations, I will pick you up around seven o'clock."

10th CHAPTER

When Saturday evening arrived, Matthew picked up Michelle at her mother's house and drove to the Spicy Lemongrass Bistro, located a few blocks away from the boardwalk on a busy intersection. The interior of the restaurant consisted of a clean modern design with halogen lighting above each table. After a friendly hostess greeted the missionaries, they were seated in a semi-circular booth near the back.

"This menu looks so complex," Matthew said. "I wouldn't know how to pronounce any of these entrées, much less know what I'm ordering."

"It's pretty simple," Michelle said. "Pho is a flat, rectangular rice noodle, so there are only three options: pho soup, pho salad or a variety of pho main dishes. If you want, I will order for us."

"What were you thinking sounds good?" Matthew asked.

"I was thinking about two vegetarian spring rolls for an appetizer," Michelle said, "but to save money, we could skip the spring rolls and order a beef, chicken and tofu main course, because I know you're going to be hungry. The beef dish has pho noodles, tender slices of beef, peanuts, bean sprouts and fresh herbs. All the dishes come with a variety of sauces, so we could ask for extra plates and share all three dishes. Please don't worry about the bill, it's my treat tonight."

"That's kind of you," Matthew said. "It has been difficult for me not having any money."

"I was very touched watching you take forty dollars out of your pocket and give it to our friends the other day," Michelle said.

"Maybe I could make my own cardboard sign and stand on the street corner in front of the Rescue Mission," Matthew said. "I would use a white poster board with bold letters that said, 'Please Support My Homeless Ministry.'"

"Another option would be to crash Monica's fund-raising party at the art gallery dressed as a homeless man holding a tin can and ringing a bell," Michelle said.

"It feels like it's taking forever to even ask Monica if she's interested," Matthew said.

"Every time I greet our guests at the front door, I collect a few more signs," Michelle said. "So let's keep praying, collect more signs and stand on God's Word that says, 'The laborer deserves to be paid.'"[104]

"Before we discuss the rapture, I wanted to clarify a few basic principles about Sacred Scripture," Matthew said. "Because the Bible was written over two thousand years ago to a primarily Jewish audience, it's important to study and understand the author's intended message to the original audience. Once we understand the author's intended message to a primarily Jewish audience, we can apply that message to our lives.

"A good example of how our modern-day pastors and television evangelists have been twisting God's Word out of context comes from the Letter of Paul to the Romans. In chapter ten, Saint Paul says, 'Everyone who calls on the name of the Lord shall be saved.'[105] When someone takes this verse out of context from the rest of the paragraph, and out of context with the rest of the chapter, and out of context from the source that Saint Paul is quoting, the verse by itself could mean almost anything to anyone.

"It is very unfortunate that many of our modern-day television evangelists use this verse to imply just how easy it is to be saved. They say all a person needs to do is call on the Lord's name and that person shall be saved, meaning they are guaranteed to go to heaven. At the opposite extreme, Jesus says the road that leads to everlasting life is hard and narrow and few people will find it, but our modern-day television evangelists say all you need to do is make a simple call, and everybody shall be saved.

"When we study the paragraph from where this verse is taken, we see quotation marks surrounding the verse, because Saint Paul is quoting an Old Testament source in his letter to the Romans. In my Bible, the footnotes read, 'Joel 2:32.' Now that we know the source that Saint Paul is quoting, we need to go back and read the entire second chapter of Joel to understand the original meaning to the intended audience. Once we understand that, we can bring that meaning forward into Paul's letter to the Romans.

"When we study the second chapter of Joel, the prophet was describing a time in history when God will pour out his spirit on all flesh, meaning that the kingdom of heaven will be available to all people, both Jews and Gentiles. This was a big deal for the Jewish religious leaders at the time because the Jews were considered God's chosen race.[106] It was inconceivable for the Jews to consider that an unclean Gentile could enter the kingdom of heaven.

"We can see this attitude in other books of the Bible. For example, when God called the Apostle Peter to deliver the Gospel message to Cornelius' household, he gave him a rooftop vision of a tarp coming down out of heaven filled with all kinds of four-footed creatures and reptiles. When Peter heard the Lord's voice telling him to eat, he responded by saying, 'By no means, Lord; for I have never eaten anything that is profane or unclean.'[107] After receiving the vision three times, he heard the Lord's voice telling him, 'What God has made clean, you must not call profane.'[108]

"When Peter was still trying to figure out the meaning of the vision, messengers from Cornelius' household appeared at the front gate looking for him. The Holy

Spirit spoke to Peter, saying, 'Three men are searching for you. Now get up, go down, and go with them without hesitation; for I have sent them.'[109] After following the men back to Caesarea, Peter entered Cornelius' house and said to them, 'You yourselves know that it is unlawful for a Jew to associate with or to visit a Gentile; but God has shown me that I should not call anyone profane or unclean.'[110] After Peter delivered the Gospel message to Cornelius' household, the Holy Spirit fell on all those who heard the word, and Peter was 'astounded that the gift of the Holy Spirit had been poured out even on the Gentiles.'[111]

"During this same period of time in church history, Saint Paul was addressing an audience in Rome that held similar beliefs. That's why in his letter to the Romans he wrote, 'For there is no distinction between Jew and Greek; the same Lord is Lord of all and is generous to all who call on him.'[112] After Saint Paul establishes that the kingdom of heaven is now available to both Jews and Gentiles, he quotes the Prophet Joel, and by doing so, he is essentially saying that even the Prophet Joel described a time in history when the kingdom of heaven would be open to everyone, both Jews and Gentiles.

"So the proper meaning of Romans, chapter ten, verse thirteen is that the kingdom of heaven is now open to both Jews and Gentiles. This is the meaning from the Prophet Joel, and this is the meaning that makes sense with the rest of the paragraph. Saint Paul would never say the only requirement for being saved is calling on the Lord's name, because that would conflict with everything else that he wrote about in his letters to the newly established churches."

"That makes a lot of sense," Michelle said. "There's a passage of Scripture from the Second Letter of Peter that says, 'No prophecy of Scripture is a matter of one's own interpretation.'[113] Then at the end of the letter, Saint Peter says, 'Our beloved brother Paul wrote to you according to the wisdom given him, speaking of this as he does in all his letters. There are some things in them hard to understand, which the ignorant and unstable twist to their own destruction, as they do the other Scriptures.'"[114]

"That's the first point I wanted to make," Matthew said. "Anytime you see quotation marks surrounding text in the New Testament, it's important to look at the footnotes in your Bible to find out where in the Old Testament that sentence is being quoted from. Once you know the Old Testament source, it's important to read that entire chapter to fully understand what is being said to the original audience. Once you understand the original meaning of the quote from the Old Testament, you can bring that meaning forward and insert it into the New Testament passage. When you do this, all of Saint Paul's writings will make perfect sense."

"Saint Paul would never take a passage of Scripture from the Old Testament, twist the meaning out of context, and then insert a distorted meaning into one of his letters," Michelle said.

"Exactly," Matthew said as the waiter approached the table with the food.

After praying a blessing over the meal, Michelle said, "This looks delicious and smells so good." Then she took her chopsticks and dipped a piece of tofu into the spicy hot garlic sauce.

"The other clarification that I wanted to make concerns the Book of Revelation," Matthew said. "Catholics believe that God is the author of Sacred Scripture and that all Scripture is inspired by God.[115] We also believe that the Bible faithfully teaches the truth that God wanted to impart to humanity without error. We also believe the Bible is complete and that we are not expecting any additional revelation that needs to be added to the Bible.[116]

"Because the Book of Revelation is considered to be an apocalyptic style of literature, it uses poetic language, symbolism involving numbers, and strange beasts that captivate the reader's imagination. A good example of the Book of Revelation's use of symbolic numbers comes from the one hundred and forty-four thousand saints who have been marked with a seal.[117] Is this a literal number of twelve thousand Jews from the twelve tribes of Israel who have been marked with the seal of redemption, or does this number represent an indefinite amount, or does this number represent completeness?"

"I'm not sure what it means," Michelle said. "Jehovah's Witnesses believe in a literal interpretation where only one hundred and forty-four thousand souls will go to heaven as spirit guides, and the rest of their church members will live in the New Jerusalem."

"Because we don't have a codebook to decipher all the symbolic representation described in the Book of Revelation, the Catholic Church has based our end-time eschatology on the words of Christ contained in the Gospel of Matthew.[118] Basically, our world will continue to grow more and more evil, and after we pass through a period of time known as the Great Tribulation, our Heavenly Father will determine a day and the hour for the Second Coming of Christ.

"Jesus describes this event in the Gospel of Matthew by saying, 'Because of the increase of lawlessness, the love of many will grow cold. But the one who endures to the end will be saved. And this good news of the kingdom will be proclaimed throughout the world, as a testimony to all the nations; and then the end will come.'[119]

"Once Jesus returns and fulfills all the prophecies of Scripture regarding his Second Coming, that is the end of our world. The Apostle Peter makes the same point by saying, 'The day of the Lord will come like a thief, and then the heavens will pass away with a loud noise, and the elements will be dissolved with fire, and the earth and everything that is done on it will be disclosed.'[120]

"After the heavens pass away with a loud noise and the elements are dissolved with fire, we will en-ter the Great Judgment as described in the Book of

Revelation.[121] According to the words of Christ, 'When the Son of Man comes in his glory, and all the angels with him, then he will sit on the throne of his glory. All the nations will be gathered before him, and he will separate people one from another as a shepherd separates the sheep from the goats.'[122] The goats will enter into eternal punishment and the righteous into eternal life."

"What about the rapture?" Michelle asked as she filled Matthew's cup with more ginseng tea.

"When Saint Paul wrote about the rapture in his First Letter to the Thessalonians, he was addressing a group of Christians who were concerned about their grandparents' salvation," Matthew said. "Because many of their ancestors died before Jesus was even born, Saint Paul assured them by saying, 'For this we declare to you by the word of the Lord, that we who are alive, who are left until the coming of the Lord, will by no means precede those who have died. For the Lord himself, with a cry of command, with the archangel's call and with the sound of God's trumpet, will descend from heaven, and the dead in Christ will rise first. Then we who are alive, who are left, will be caught up in the clouds together with them to meet the Lord in the air; and so we will be with the Lord forever.'[123]

"If the end of the world occurred tonight, then those who have died and are awaiting the resurrection would rise first; then afterward, we would ascend through the roof of this restaurant to meet the Lord in the air. So in a way, Catholics do believe in the rapture, but we don't believe in the *Left Behind* series theology, because it would require a third coming of Christ."

"What do you mean?" Michelle asked.

"I realize the *Left Behind* novels are very popular in many mainstream Christian churches, but if Christ returned tonight, and all true believers were caught up in the air to meet him during the rapture, with the rest of humanity left behind to live through several more years of tribulation, then Jesus would need to make a third appearance to deal with all the people who converted to Christianity during that period of time. Because Sacred Scripture doesn't support a third coming of Christ, we should not base our end-time eschatology on a fictional novel."

"What do you think will happen to all the men and women from the Old Testament who never had a chance to hear the Gospel message?" Michelle asked as she folded up her napkin.

"In the Gospel of John, there's a passage that says, 'No one has ascended into heaven except the one who descended from heaven, the Son of Man.'[124] Many Christians will use this verse to say that nobody can enter heaven until after the Great Judgment. If these Christians would continue reading a little further, in the fifth chapter of John, Jesus says, 'Very truly, I tell you, the hour is coming, and is now here, when the dead will hear the voice of the Son of God, and those who hear will live. Do not be astonished at this; for the hour is coming when all who are in their graves will hear his voice and will come out—those who have done good, to the resurrection of life, and those who have done evil, to the resurrection of condemnation.'[125]

"This passage of Scripture was fulfilled after Jesus died on the cross for the forgiveness of our sins. The Catholic Church teaches that while Jesus was still inside the tomb, he descended into the abode of the dead for three days so that he could proclaim the Gospel message to those who had already passed away.[126] The Lord's three-day journey to the abode of the dead is described in the Gospel of Matthew where Jesus says, 'For just as Jonah was three days and three nights in the belly of the sea monster, so for three days and three nights the Son of Man will be in the heart of the earth.'[127] This teaching also comes from the First Letter of Peter where the Apostle says, 'The gospel was proclaimed even to the dead.'[128]

"So to answer your question about what's going to happen to the Old Testament saints who died before Jesus was born, they already had the opportunity to hear the Gospel message directly from Jesus. According to the Gospel of John, those who are righteous will enter the resurrection of life, and those who have rejected the Gospel message will end up in the lake of fire for all eternity."[129]

"My greatest concern with the Catholic Church is that everybody is always attacking it," Michelle said. "At least once a month, I hear several minutes of a preacher's sermon that has been allocated to describing just how great my own church is and just how far from the truth all the other Christian denominations have fallen. The Catholic Church must have a big red target on its back, because it has always been the main focus of every attack."

"I'm not sure how to respond to that concern," Matthew said, "except to say that the Catholic Church is the only Christian denomination that can trace its roots back to the first-century Christian church. For more than twelve hundred years, there was only one church—the Holy Catholic Apostolic Church—and after the Protestant Reformation occurred in the fifteenth century, we now have over ten thousand different religious denominations that continue to attack each other, divide into separate groups and start their own religious sects."

"I still don't understand why the Catholic Church will not allow us to have a beach wedding," Michelle said.

"I was going to look into how to acquire an exemption," Matthew said, "but with all the explanations that I have been providing, I was hoping it wouldn't be necessary."

"I'm sorry," Michelle said. "I have always envisioned a beach wedding on a tropical island overlooking the ocean. It doesn't have to be a tropical island. Many hotels in Cancun, Playa del Carmen, or even Puerto Vallarta specialize in beach weddings, and all those hotels can provide accommodations for our guests."

"I will ask Clergyman O'Connor how we can apply for the exemption," Matthew said. "In the meantime, what do you want to do about Amber? I was thinking we don't need to wait until next week to take her shopping, because we know where she lives. We can stop by her outdoor sign anytime we want to see if she's available."

"That's a good idea," Michelle said as she watched the waiter collect the dishes and drop off the check.

"Let me get that," Matthew said as he picked up the check from the table before Michelle could look at it. "I know it was your treat tonight, but I was thinking of selling my mountain bike."

"You love that bike," Michelle said.

"I know, but think of all the homeless people we could help with the proceeds," Matthew said.

11th CHAPTER

The following day, when the missionaries stopped by the Rescue Mission to see if Amber was around, they found her underneath her outdoor sign drinking a pint of peach schnapps.

"So what's your favorite drink?" Matthew asked as he sat down next to her.

Because Amber was trying to hide the bottle in her backpack, Matthew said, "Do you like whiskey on the rocks, dark beers or are you more of a rum and tropical fruit girl?"

"I like sweet drinks," Amber said.

"Because you were so kind and helped us pick up trash the other day, we wanted to take you shopping at the thrift store this afternoon," Michelle said.

"Not today," Amber said.

"Are you sure?" Matthew asked. "You still have a ten-dollar credit with us, and it could very easily buy some warm blankets, a sleeping bag, a winter coat or even some new clothes."

"I need new clothes," Amber said.

"Just let us know when you're ready," Matthew said as he stood up and started walking away.

"Wait a second," Amber said. "Where are you going?"

"I have to get back to work," Matthew said.

"When are you coming back?" Amber asked.

"How about we meet you here tomorrow afternoon at one o'clock?" Matthew said.

"You know where to find me," Amber said.

After the missionaries walked back to Michelle's Jeep and climbed inside, she said, "I get the feeling that Amber doesn't like women. Did you see the way she was responding to you? As if she would do anything you asked."

"We may be able to use that to our advantage," Matthew said, "especially when it comes time to visit the Sacrament of Reconciliation."

* * *

During the next several weeks, the missionaries continued to stop by and visit with Amber whenever they were in the area. After taking her shopping at the thrift store, they were able to develop a deeper friendship with her and learn more about her past. On other occasions, they would bring her granola bars and fresh fruit; and other times, they would take her out to lunch after the chapel service.

When Valentine's Day arrived, Michelle parked her Jeep in front of the Rescue Mission and unloaded three grocery-sized bags filled with loving works of art. Every card had been carefully crafted with a personal message of encouragement and decorated with markers, glitter and crayons.

"How do you want to handle the distribution?" Matthew asked.

"I made a CD of my favorite Christian love songs," Michelle said. "I think we should play soft music while you distribute cards on one side of the aisle, and I will distribute cards on the other side."

When the room reached the maximum seating capacity, Michelle closed the outer doors while Matthew said to the audience, "Because today is Valentine's Day, we have a special gift to share with you. We wanted to bestow on you a gift of love from God's heart to your heart, so the students at Centerfield Elementary School made everyone a love letter on God's behalf."

When Matthew had finished speaking, Michelle started playing the CD and said, "Let's take our time and look everyone in the eyes as we pick out the perfect card before presenting it to that person."

After all the cards had been distributed, Matthew said to the audience, "If anyone wants to get their picture taken holding your Valentine's Day card, please form a line in the back of the chapel. We wanted to give your pictures to the schoolchildren as a way of saying thank you for sharing God's extravagant love with us."

After Matthew made the announcement, about thirty people stood up and headed toward the back of the room so that Michelle could take their pictures. While Michelle was coordinating group photos, Matthew said to the audience, "Please turn with me to the Gospel of John. In the seventeenth chapter, Jesus said that the Father loved him before the foundation of the world.[130]

"Think about that for a second. Before the world existed, God's love was present. A good description of God's love has been described in the First Letter of John where the Apostle says, 'God is love, and those who abide in love abide in God.'[131] We can also see the theme of God's love running through the entire Bible. For example, in the Book of Genesis, God created Adam and Eve in the Garden of Eden for fellowship.

"The Bible says that God used to visit his beloved children during the time of the evening breeze.[132] God used to walk hand-in-hand with Adam and Eve because he loved them very much. We can also see God's love in the Ten Commandments when he describes himself as a jealous lover.[133]

"When Jesus gave us the greatest commandment, he invited us to enter into a love affair with God by saying, 'You shall love the Lord your God with all your heart, and with all your soul, and with all your mind, and with all your strength.'[134] In the center of the Bible, there's a love story called the Song of Solomon about a man and woman who love each other very much. In a symbolic way, this story represents God's love for us.

"Then in the Book of Isaiah, God declares his love for humanity by saying, 'You shall be a crown of beauty in the hand of the Lord, and a royal diadem in the hand of your God. You shall no more be termed Forsaken, and your land shall no more be termed Desolate; but you shall be called My Delight Is in Her, and your land Married; for the Lord delights in you, and your land shall be married. For as a young man marries a young woman, so shall your builder marry you, and as the bridegroom rejoices over the bride, so shall your God rejoice over you.'[135]

"God's desire to enter into a marriage union with us is fulfilled in the Book of Revelation during the marriage of the Lamb. In the nineteenth chapter, there was the sound of thunder crying out Hallelujah! 'For the marriage of the Lamb has come, and his bride has made herself ready.'[136] The bride of Christ described in the Book of Revelation is the holy city Jerusalem coming down out of heaven from God.[137]

"So you see, from the beginning of Sacred Scripture to the end, we have a God who loves us and wants to make his home within our hearts. Jesus wants to be the lover of your soul. He wants to fill you with his peaceful presence, but he will not violate anyone's free will. You have to surrender your life to the Lord's service. You have to open your heart to Jesus in the same way that a man falls in love with a woman.

"Let me give you an example of how that works. When a man falls in love with a woman, he opens his heart and invites her presence inside of his heart. If you're a woman in the audience, the opposite of that would be true. When a woman falls in love with a man, she opens her heart and invites the man's presence inside of her heart. That's the prayer I wanted to pray with you today. Let's open our hearts to invite the presence of Jesus to dwell in us, so that we can enter into a more intimate relationship with the Blessed Trinity."

After the service, a large gathering of men and women approached the stage with a newfound sense of love and joy in their hearts, thanking the missionaries for sharing God's love with them.

* * *

Later that evening, when Matthew stopped by Mrs. Nobility's house to pick up his fiancée for the Valentine's Day dance, he rang the doorbell and was greeted by Michelle's mother, who invited him inside.

"She's still upstairs trying on different outfits," Mrs. Nobility said.

"I'm almost ready," Michelle called out from her second-story bedroom. When she walked down the stairs, she was wearing a new pair of high-heel shoes, a short black skirt, a golden-colored sleeveless halter top, and a slightly oversized bright red jacket.

"How do I look?" Michelle asked.

"That skirt is way too short," Mrs. Nobility said.

"I think you look great," Matthew said. "You can barely notice the skirt because your jacket extends past it by several inches."

"Don't wait up for us," Michelle said, kissing her mother good night.

"It was good seeing you," Matthew said. "I will have her back home before midnight."

When the missionaries arrived at the hotel, they were greeted at the front desk and directed toward the grand ballroom, which was filled with guests. In the center of the room, hanging over a table with refreshments, was a white banner with golden font that displayed the name "Christian Singles International."

At the entrance of the grand ballroom, the missionaries were greeted by a group of volunteers who were helping guests snap on wristbands in exchange for a ten-dollar entrance fee.

"I thought this was a Jclub event," Matthew said to one of the volunteers.

"Daniel has been making a lot of changes," Michelle said as she took a twenty-dollar bill from her purse and handed it to the cashier.

"You would think they would let us in for free," Matthew said.

"Look over there," Michelle said. "Daniel and Rebecca are dancing in the center of the floor. Let's go out there and join them."

When Daniel and Rebecca recognized their friends, they stopped dancing and exchanged hugs. "It has been a long time," Daniel said. "How have you been doing?"

"Working with the homeless has been a constant learning experience for me," Matthew said. "It's a very challenging environment; and at times, the ministry is extremely difficult, but it's such a thrill to feel the power of God flowing through us and into the lives of others."

"Michelle has been sharing the stories of changed lives that you have witnessed," Daniel said.

"Why did you change the name of Jclub?" Matthew asked.

"We opened a new division for adults called Christian Singles International," Daniel said. "We are still operating Jclub for high school students with the help of a growing network of youth pastors."

"That makes sense," Matthew said. "I like the new name. It sounds very impressive, and it was probably a good idea to keep the high school students separate from the adults."

"It felt like the high school memberships were hindering adult participation, so after we separated them into two separate divisions, the sales have increased exponentially," Daniel said.

"Did Michelle mention her idea of hosting a fund-raising event at Monica's art gallery?" Matthew asked.

"She told me all about it, and we are in full support of your efforts," Daniel said. "I have been wanting to talk with you about using my airline miles to help you book a free flight to Africa. My parents are constantly flying back and forth to Israel using free miles, so I was thinking you could use some of my miles to book your flight to Africa."

"That would be great," Matthew said.

"We would have to call the airline to verify the details," Daniel said. "It will take about eighty thousand miles to book a round-trip ticket to Africa, but the good news is that many credit card companies are offering free miles just for opening an account. If the airline will allow me to pay for a ticket in your name, we can book the flight anytime you want.

"The only problem is that the flights where you can use free miles usually have longer connection times. You may have to fly to New York, with a layover in London and Egypt, and then to your final destination in Africa."

"That wouldn't be a problem," Matthew said. "It would give us an opportunity to see the world."

"For Michelle's ticket, I was thinking about opening a credit card in Rebecca's name," Daniel said. "If we only need to spend three thousand dollars to get fifty thousand bonus miles, we could do that in a few weeks. We have been spending thousands of dollars every month on Christian radio advertisements, so we could have an unlimited amount of miles for you and Michelle to travel back and forth anytime you wanted."

"That would be such a blessing," Matthew said.

As the missionaries were speaking, a volunteer approached Daniel and said, "The hotel manager would like to speak with you."

"Please tell him that I will meet him in the front lobby in five minutes," Daniel said.

"It sounds like you have to go," Matthew said.

"We have to clear the room by eleven o'clock tonight," Daniel said. "A business expo needs the space early tomorrow morning, and the hotel staff wants us to vacate the premises early so they can set up the tables and chairs."

"Do you need any help cleaning up this evening?" Matthew asked.

"It's all taken care of," Daniel said. "If you have some free time, I really miss seeing you. I know a lot of other members feel the same way. We used to hang out all the time together in the church basement eating lox and bagels with cream cheese. We should get together for fellowship sometime very soon."

"You're right," Matthew said. "I'm sorry for being so distant. I'll call you next week so that we can set something up."

At the end of the evening, after Matthew spent several hours reconnecting with all his old friends, he approached Michelle and said, "Would you like to join me for the last slow dance of the evening?"

"I thought you would never ask," Michelle said, wrapping her arms around his waist.

"This night has been such a blessing for me," Matthew said. "I needed to get away from the homeless for a while and to reconnect with my old friends."

"A lot of people love and respect you for all the work you did in building up Jclub," Michelle said. "Without your involvement, none of us would be here this evening."

"Thank you," Matthew said, "that means a lot to me."

* * *

When the missionaries were driving home that evening, Michelle said, "When you were getting reacquainted with all your friends, Rebecca started asking me questions about our relationship."

"What did you tell her?" Matthew asked.

"I told her everything," Michelle said. "We also spoke about the difference between Christian courtship, secular dating and the betrothal process. I think she was interested in our relationship because her courtship with Daniel is starting to get more serious."

"They make such a beautiful couple," Matthew said. "Do you remember how we spent all week praying and fasting before we got engaged?"

"How could I forget!" Michelle said. "It was such a powerful experience."

"I'm wondering if we should set aside another week for a blender fast and invite Daniel and Rebecca to join us again," Matthew said.

"Are you concerned that it's too soon for them to get engaged?" Michelle asked.

"I want to spend a week drawing closer to God," Matthew said. "I would like to ask the Lord some very specific questions about our ministry efforts."

"What kind of questions?" Michelle asked.

"Daniel told me we could use his airline miles to book a flight to Africa," Matthew said. "He's also working on a way to acquire a free ticket for you, but before we can research the flights, we need to know what country in Africa the Lord wants us to visit.

"The first question I wanted to ask the Lord concerns the timing of our trip. Maybe God wants us to focus on the homeless ministry for several more years, and then go to Africa; or maybe our work with the homeless was only a temporary stepping stone so that we could learn some important lessons about preaching to a hostile audience.

"I'm not sure, but during the fast, I want to ask God if I'm called to do more homeless work or if I'm being called to Africa. If I'm being called to Africa, I need to know what country so we can book our flights."

"I'm ready to start fasting whenever you are," Michelle said after Matthew pulled into her mom's driveway and gave her a long hug and kiss good night.

* * *

The next day, Matthew called Michelle and said, "Do you have time to make a conference call to Daniel and Rebecca?"

"I already spoke to Rebecca this morning," Michelle said. "She was excited to embark on a holy week with us, and she said Daniel was in full support. If we start the blender fast on the last Tuesday of the month, it would put the event at Monica's art gallery on the fifth day of the fast, which would be perfect timing for my schedule."

"That works for me too," Matthew said.

* * *

A few days after the missionaries started fasting, Matthew received a call from Chaplain Hemingway at the Rescue Mission. He said, "I'm sorry to call you so early, but Amber was attacked last night in the parking lot. She had been arguing with some guys earlier that day and we think one of them came back at night and tried to kill her when she was sleeping."

"Oh, no! Is she okay?" Matthew asked.

"The perpetrator used a cinder block," Chaplain Hemingway said. "Amber lay unconscious all night wrapped up in a bloody blanket. The guys who found her said they could see her brain exposed through the large gash in her skull."

"Where is she now?" Matthew asked.

"After we called the police, the paramedics arrived and took her away early this morning," the Chaplain said. "I tried calling several hospitals in the area, but nobody would give me any information."

"I will get right on it and let you know when I find her," Matthew said.

After getting off the phone, Matthew jumped in his 4Runner and drove to Lakeside Regional Hospital. When he arrived, he asked a nurse who was working in the emergency room if Amber Rose Thunderhawk had been admitted earlier that morning.

"We don't have any patients by that name," the nurse said.

"I'm a chapel provider at the Rescue Mission," Matthew said. "Amber is a Native American woman who I have been working with for several months. She was attacked early this morning, and I need to find her."

"We have a Jane Doe who was admitted with head trauma," the nurse said. "Because of the suspicious nature surrounding her injuries, I'm going to need to see your identification and get my supervisor's approval for any visits."

After Matthew gave the nurse his driver's license, he took a seat in the waiting area and began praying for Amber's recovery. About fifteen minutes later, a security guard approached him to return his driver's license. He said, "I'm sorry for the delay. My supervisor verified your identity as a chapel service provider at the Rescue Mission, so he placed your name on the approved visitor list. Please follow me to the intensive care unit to see if you can identify Jane Doe."

12th CHAPTER

When Matthew entered the room, he was immediately confronted with the seriousness of the situation. Amber's face was swollen so badly that he could barely recognize her. She had a broken nose and heavy black marks under both eyes. The nurses had shaved her head so the surgeons could repair the trauma to her skull. The heavy black stitches they used looked like train tracks running across the side of her head in a semi-circular pattern.

"That's her," Matthew said. "Her name is Amber Rose Thunderhawk."

"Thank you," the security guard said.

After the security guard left the room, a nurse entered and said, "Right now, she's on a ventilator. Every couple of hours, we take her off to see if she can breathe on her own. So far, she has failed both tests."

"Thank you for saving her life," Matthew said. "I will come back tomorrow to see how she's doing."

When Matthew left the hospital, he sat down on a

park bench near a water fountain to make several phone calls. After calling Chaplain Hemingway with an update, he called Michelle and told her what had happened.

"I'm so very sorry," Michelle said. "Is there anything I can do?"

"All we can do at this time is pray and wait to see if Amber makes it through the night," Matthew said.

"How are you feeling?" Michelle asked.

"It was very difficult for me to see her like that," Matthew said. "She was loaded full of tubes in her arms and down her throat. There was even a shiny brass fitting on the top of her head. The surgeons placed it there to prevent pressure from building up inside her skull.

"There was also a terrible stench of death in the room. It made me so sick it felt like I was going to vomit. As difficult as it was for me to see her like that, another part of me is angry because we have given her many opportunities to stop drinking and get her life together. All she needed to do was check herself into a detox facility, and we would have rented her an apartment where she would have been safe at night. Instead, she made countless decisions to get drunk and cause everybody around her a lot of problems."

"Although the situation is extremely sad and painful at this moment, God is still able to accomplish his divine will in her life," Michelle said.

"She can't even breathe on her own," Matthew said. "The nurses don't think she is going to live another twenty-four hours."

"Ever since we met Amber, I have been praying for her sobriety and salvation," Michelle said. "As sad and painful as it is right now, maybe this is God's way of helping her get clean and sober. If a cinder block to the head is the only thing that will help her stop drinking, then God in his loving kindness will give Amber all the spiritual blessings that she needs to make a full recovery."

"I told the nurses I would come back tomorrow morning to check on her," Matthew said.

"I would like to come with you," Michelle said.

"I'm not sure they will let you in to see her," Matthew said. "The police are still looking for the perpetrator, and they needed to verify my identity with the Rescue Mission before putting my name on the approved visitor list. Let's see if Amber makes it through the night, then I will ask the nurses about their visitation policy tomorrow morning."

* * *

The following morning, when Matthew called Michelle to give her an update on Amber's condition, he said, "It doesn't look good. She still can't breathe on her own, and her condition continues to deteriorate."

"During my quiet time with the Lord this morning, I received several Scripture passages about Amber's situation that I wanted to share with you," Michelle said.

"Go ahead," Matthew said.

"I think we need to discuss them in person," Michelle said. "My mom is out shopping with her friends this morning. Would you like to come over for some orange juice?"

"That would be great," Matthew said.

When Matthew arrived, Michelle greeted him with a hug and kiss, then she said, "I'm so happy we are fasting this week. I had an incredible encounter with the Lord this morning when he was showing me all of his healing verses. I can't wait to share them with you."

"I'm ready whenever you are," Matthew said, taking a seat at the dining room table.

"The first verse comes from the Gospel of Luke when the Lord sent seventy missionaries to various towns in pairs of two," Michelle said. "He told them to cure the sick and say to them, 'The kingdom of God has come near to you.'[138]

"The instructions the Lord gave the disciples were not optional. They were a requirement. The missionaries were expected to cure the sick. It is also important to note that two missionaries were working together as a team, not just one person working by himself.

"The second passage comes from the Gospel of Luke when the Lord healed Peter's mother-in-law. Because she was lying in bed with a fever, the Lord stood over her and 'rebuked the fever, and it left her.'[139] The word *rebuke* means a verbal command was issued. Jesus addressed the root cause of the problem and commanded the sickness to get out of her body.

"The third passage comes from the Gospel of Mark where Jesus says, 'Truly I tell you, if you say to this mountain, "Be taken up and thrown into the sea," and if you do not doubt in your heart, but believe that what you say will come to pass, it will be done for you. So I tell you, whatever you ask for in prayer, believe that you have received it, and it will be yours.'[140]

"To activate the power of this Scripture passage, we need to issue a verbal command. We have to speak directly to the mountain of difficulty and hardships that Amber is facing, and believe in our hearts that what we have spoken will come to pass.

"The fourth passage comes from the Gospel of Matthew where Jesus says, 'For truly I tell you, if you have faith the size of a mustard seed, you will say to this mountain, "Move from here to there," and it will move; and nothing will be impossible for you.'[141]

"To activate the power of this Scripture passage, we have to have faith the size of a mustard seed along with the assurance and expectations that Amber will make a full recovery.

"The fifth passage also comes from the Gospel of Matthew where Jesus says, 'Again, truly I tell you, if two of you agree on earth about anything you ask, it will be done for you by my Father in heaven. For where two or three are gathered in my name, I am there among them.'[142]

"Notice in this passage that two people are required and that both parties need to agree on a desired outcome. It will not be possible to agree upon a desired outcome if one person thinks the situation is hopeless while the other person is expecting a full recovery.

"During my prayer time this morning, I was grateful that you have already prepared me for what we will encounter when we enter Amber's hospital room—the stench of death, a swollen face, a broken nose, tubes stuck down her throat and a ventilator machine making strange noises—but we have to look past all those distractions with love in our hearts.

"We have to see Amber in a fully healed state of beauty and perfection. We have to believe in that reality, and through the power of God's Spirit, which dwells in our hearts, we have to speak into Amber's situation in a way that will bring about her healing."

"I have another verse from the Book of James that we can add to your list," Matthew said. "'Are any among you sick? They should call for the elders of the church and have them pray over them, anointing them with oil in the name of the Lord. The prayer of faith will save the sick, and the Lord will raise them up; and anyone who has committed sins will be forgiven. Therefore confess your sins to one another, and pray for one another, so that you may be healed.'[143]

"I was also thinking we should anoint Amber with oil and address the issue of sin in our prayers of intercession on her behalf. I'm also sorry for agreeing with the heightened security fears that the hospital projected on me regarding the approved visitor list. Although you wanted to come with me this morning, a part of me wanted to protect you from the heartache you would experience upon entering her room. Although I wanted your help, I also wanted to protect you."

"Maybe it's good that we didn't go down there early this morning for several reasons," Michelle said. "If we did, we probably wouldn't be having this conversation right now, and I still don't think we're ready to pray effectively."

"Why do you say that?" Matthew asked.

"According to the fifth healing Scripture, we not only have to envision a desired result, but we have to agree upon a desired result," Michelle said. "Jesus says, 'If two of you agree on earth about anything you ask, it will be done for you by my Father in heaven.'[144]

"Right now, we haven't agreed upon a mutually desired result for Amber's situation so that we can effectively ask for it in prayer. I would like to see a vision of your faith that has the power to move mountains, but because I can't see your vision of faith for Amber's situation, you are going to have to describe it for me."

"Do you want to hear about it now or on the way to the hospital?" Matthew asked.

"Let's go," Michelle said.

"We also need to stop by my apartment to get the anointing oil," Matthew said as they rushed out the front door.

After Matthew picked up the bottle of anointing oil at his apartment, Michelle said, "When it comes time to pass through the security checkpoint, let's not make a big deal about the approved visitors list. Let's denounce all fears before we arrive and fill our hearts with the faith and confidence we need to walk right past the security checkpoint.

"There shouldn't be any problems with us entering Amber's room together, because I'm your fiancée; and as your fiancée, I have been by your side as a chapel service provider at the Rescue Mission for as long as you have. In addition, I met Amber and made friends with her and promised to take her shopping long before you even knew who she was."

"There's not going to be any problems at the security checkpoint," Matthew said. "We are on a mission from God, and we are going to flow with the power and presence of Christ himself."

* * *

When the missionaries arrived at Lakeside Regional Hospital, they walked right past the security checkpoint and greeted the nurses in the intensive care unit as if they were best of friends. After approaching Amber's station, Matthew took a bottle of anointing oil out of his pocket. After looking around to make sure none of the nurses were looking, he anointed Amber's forehead and hands in the name of the Father, Son and Holy Spirit.

Matthew began his prayer by acknowledging his own sinfulness, then started to intercede on Amber's behalf by praising God for his great love and mercy. After pouring out his heart for several minutes, Michelle continued the prayer by describing Amber as a beautiful, talented and powerful woman of God in perfect health;

who was not only clean and sober but also filled with the Holy Spirit and serving the Lord in full-time ministry.

When the missionaries had finished praying for Amber, the terrible stench of death that filled the room had completely disappeared, and they experienced a tremendous sense of peace and joy in their hearts.

To be continued in *Missionaries—Volume Three*
The Rural African Village Adventure

Notes

Excerpts from the *Catechism of the Catholic Church* are quoted from the character's memory and are based on the English translation of the *Catechism of the Catholic Church* for use in the United States of America, © 1994, United States Catholic Conference, Inc.— Libreria Editrice Vaticana. English translation of the *Catechism of the Catholic Church*: Modifications from the Editio Typica copyright © 1997, United States Catholic Conference, Inc.—Libreria Editrice Vaticana. Used with permission. All rights reserved.

Interior illustrations by NightCafe Studio Art Generator. All rights reserved.

1. *Catechism of the Catholic Church*: 1633–1637 & *Code of Canon Law*: 1125.

2. *Code of Canon Law*: 1130–1133.

3. Job 1:1–3.

4. Job 1:10.

5. Job 1:18–19.

6. Job 2:7.

7. Luke 13:11–16.

8. Matthew 17:14–21.

9. John 10:10.

10. Job 1:22.

11. Job 42:12–17.

12. Luke 15:11–32.

13. Luke 15:13.

14. Ephesians 5:18.

15. Luke 15:30.

16. Luke 15:14.

17. Luke 15:16.

18. Luke 15:17.

Notes

19. Luke 15:17–19.
20. Luke 15:22–24.
21. Zechariah 2:5.
22. Deuteronomy 18:10–12.
23. John 10:10.
24. *Catechism of the Catholic Church*: 830 & 857.
25. Titus 1:5.
26. Matthew 16:18–19.
27. Acts 15:1–2.
28. Acts 15:28–29.
29. The Nicene Creed.
30. 1 Corinthians 4:15–17.
31. Matthew 23:9.
32. 1 Timothy 1:2.
33. 1 Timothy 5:17.
34. Matthew 23:9–12.
35. Romans 8:24.
36. Philippians 2:12.
37. Luke 14:27.
38. Matthew 24:13.
39. 1 Corinthians 9:24–27.
40. Hebrews 10:26–27.
41. Matthew 7:13–14.
42. John 3:5.
43. Titus 3:5.
44. *Catechism of the Catholic Church*: 1265.
45. *Catechism of the Catholic Church*: 1250 & 1272.
46. *Catechism of the Catholic Church*: 1254.
47. Acts 2:37.
48. Acts 2:38–39.
49. Luke 1:59.
50. Genesis 17:10 & Genesis 17:12.
51. Acts 16:13–15.
52. Acts 16:33.
53. Colossians 2:11–12.

Notes

54. 1 Samuel 1:27–28 & 1 Samuel 2:11.

55. Luke 1:15.

56. *Catechism of the Catholic Church*: 1272–1274; Ephesians 1:13–14, Ephesians 4:30 & 2 Corinthians 1:22.

57. *Catechism of the Catholic Church*: 1254–1255.

58. 2 Corinthians 13:5.

59. Revelation 2:4–5.

60. Revelation 1:20.

61. Revelation 3:1–3.

62. 1 Corinthians 1:10.

63. Matthew 25:31–46 & 1 John 3:10.

64. 1 John 5:10.

65. 1 John 4:13.

66. 1 John 2:3–4.

67. James 2:19.

68. 1 John 2:6.

69. Romans 1:20–23.

70. Genesis 1:1.

71. Genesis 2:7.

72. Genesis 1:20–21.

73. 1 John 5:16.

74. 1 John 5:17.

75. Galatians 5:21.

76. 1 Corinthians 6:9–10.

77. James 5:16.

78. Mark 2:5.

79. Mark 2:7.

80. Mark 2:9–11.

81. Matthew 9:8.

82. John 20:21–23.

83. 2 Corinthians 5:18.

84. 2 Corinthians 5:19–20.

85. *Catechism of the Catholic Church*: 783.

86. Ibid, Cf. John Paul II, *RH* 18–21.

87. Leviticus 11:45.

Notes

88. Matthew 5:48.
89. 1 Peter 1:15.
90. Revelation 21:27.
91. Hebrews 12:14.
92. 1 Corinthians 3:10–15.
93. Matthew 6:15.
94. Matthew 18:21.
95. Matthew 18:32–35.
96. Luke 12:57–59.
97. Matthew 23:27–28.
98. Matthew 22:1–10.
99. Matthew 22:12.
100. Matthew 22:13.
101. 1 Thessalonians 4:3.
102. Proverbs 6:6–11.
103. Proverbs 6:9.
104. 1 Timothy 5:18.
105. Romans 10:13.
106. 1 Peter 2:9 & Romans 9:4–5.
107. Acts 10:14.
108. Acts 10:15.
109. Acts 10:19–20.
110. Acts 10:28.
111. Acts 10:45.
112. Romans 10:12.
113. 2 Peter 1:20.
114. 2 Peter 3:15–16.
115. *Catechism of the Catholic Church*: 105–107 & 2 Timothy 3:16.
116. *Catechism of the Catholic Church*: 66.
117. Revelation 7:4–8.
118. Matthew 24:1–51 & Matthew 25:1–46.
119. Matthew 24:12–14.
120. 2 Peter 3:10.
121. Revelation 20:11–15.
122. Matthew 25:31–32.

123. 1 Thessalonians 4:15–17.
124. John 3:13.
125. John 5:25 & John 5:28–29.
126. *Catechism of the Catholic Church*: 631–637.
127. Matthew 12:40.
128. 1 Peter 4:6.
129. John 5:28–29.
130. John 17:24.
131. 1 John 4:16.
132. Genesis 3:8.
133. Exodus 20:4–6.
134. Mark 12:30.
135. Isaiah 62:3–5.
136. Revelation 19:7.
137. Revelation 21:9–10.
138. Luke 10:9.
139. Luke 4:39.
140. Mark 11:23–24.
141. Matthew 17:20.
142. Matthew 18:19–20.
143. James 5:14–16.
144. Matthew 18:19.

Missionaries
The Christian Social Club Adventure

Matthew Goodwin wants to move with God's power as a traveling missionary to Africa. Michelle Nobility wants to fulfill God's calling of love and marriage. Embark on a journey with the missionaries to discover how God's will is fulfilled when they encounter a presence of darkness far more sinister than they could have imagined.

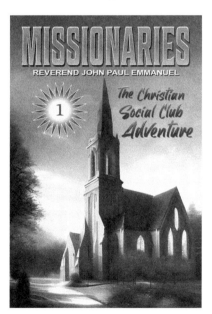

Available at your local bookstore or online.

www.ValentinePublishing.com

Missionaries
The Rural African Village Adventure

After being warned that their ministry destination was particularly dangerous, Matthew and Michelle exchange a tearful farewell with their friends and family before boarding a flight to Africa. With demonic forces lurking around every corner, the missionaries press through many trials and tribulations before obtaining the ultimate victory in Christ.

Available at your local bookstore or online.

www.ValentinePublishing.com

African Missionaries

Please consider supporting Matthew and Michelle's outreach ministry by making a tax-deductible donation to African Missionaries.

African Missionaries is a 501(c)(3) non-profit public charity that conducts mission trips to the poorest countries of the world for the purpose of spreading the Gospel message.

You can make an online donation by visiting www.ValentinePublishing.com or by sending a check to the following address:

African Missionaries
PO Box 27422
Denver, Colorado 80227

Please support our outreach ministry by distributing copies of *Missionaries, Volumes One, Two & Three* to your friends and family members.

To purchase a three-volume set, please use the following information:

Three-Volume Set	Ministry Price
One Set	$29
Two Sets	$59
Three Sets	$89

These prices include tax and free shipping within the United States. For shipments to other countries, please contact us. Thank you for your generous support.

Please mail your payment to:

Valentine Publishing House
Missionaries — Volumes One, Two & Three
PO Box 27422
Denver, Colorado 80227